French Cooking

made easy

A modern collection of simple regional cooking

Galahad Books · New York City

French Cooking made easy published by Galahad Books,
New York City

This edition published by arrangement with 'Round the World
Books Inc., New York, New York

Series designed by Margaret Verner

Additional information contributed by SOPEXA (Canada),
Foods from France.

Library of Congress Catalog Card Number: 79-87996

ISBN: 0-88365-417-2

Printed in the United States of America

Contents

France at the table

INTRODUCTION

To most people the pleasures of really good food and wine are an occasional reward in a busy life. To the French they are pleasures that really belong to daily life. Eating and drinking in France is the expression of an ancient tradition, refined over the centuries. It is a central pillar of family and social life and a serious occupation for which Frenchmen allow themselves plenty of time.

It is true that more and more snack bars are beginning to appear in the cities and that along the highways and turnpikes more roadside restaurants are being built where you can eat a quick meal that has taken no great pains to prepare. But in the provinces, eating is still what it has been for centuries in France: a sacred ritual performed with single-minded concentration and deep satisfaction.

If you are invited to lunch by a Frenchman who lives out in the provinces, you can plan to remain at the

table from half past twelve until at least four o'clock. Not only do you savor the food and wine, but the whole meal, from beginning to end, is designed as an affable and special occasion. You arise from the table, mellowed a little by the wine, at peace with life and far from your troubles.

Sunday is an important day in France. It is the day when the city dweller, who works far away from home during the week and has to content himself with a quick bite to eat at the local bistro, takes his family out to participate in the national pastime of good

eating. This is the main reason for Sunday's great exodus of cars from the cities, packed with father, mother, the small children, grown children and grandparents, whenever possible. Their destination is a restaurant in the country where the cook and the wine cellar have acquired a good reputation for dependability. In any country restaurant where there is a cook who takes his art seriously, Sunday is the climactic achievement of a week's efforts. You can be sure that the restaurant will be filled right down to the last table and that the cook has

Also in small wayside restaurant truckdrivers enjoy such specialities as escargots.

carefully ordered the exact quantity of fresh fish, vegetables, meat, game and fruit that is needed.

There is usually only one meal on the menu, but it is worked out to the finest detail. Most of the restaurants do not even give you a written menu on Sunday, you just sit down and wait for whatever comes. The large room which remains closed during the week is now open to accomodate the patrons. It has fresh flowers arranged by Madam herself, and there is extra help brought in from the village. At about twelve o'clock the room begins to fill up and by one o'clock every seat is taken; the door is then locked, a sign reading "full" is hung outside and the party begins. Though the sole entertainment is to be food and conversation, no one will leave until the black coffee and brandy have arrived to mark the end of the meal, some three and a half hours later.

The main dish of these Sunday meals is usually

chicken, a choice that would have gladdened the heart of Henry IV, King of France from 1589-1610. His great ideal was for every Frenchman to have a chicken in the pot on Sunday – an unimaginable social and economic achievement for those times. But even if all of France were to eat chicken on Sunday, it would certainly not mean that everyone ate chicken prepared in the same way. That would be even more unimaginable. From region to region chicken differs in color, taste, fragrance and aroma, character, sauce, garnishing and stuffing. You could travel throughout France for a year, or perhaps two, and eat a chicken prepared in a totally different way each Sunday.

This is one of the most enchanting aspects of French cooking: that it is actually a collection of regional dishes and cooking ideas, each one totally different in character. All the great French chefs look to each of the different regional cuisines for their inspiration. Alexandre Dumaine, one of the greatest French cooks of the last century, once confessed that when he felt that his inspiration was drying up he would go to spend a few days with his old aunts in the country. There were always a few new and exciting ideas in their kitchen.

NORMANDY

You can certainly recognize the cooking by the region from which it comes. Normandy, in the northwest of France, is a region of lush green fields where fat cattle graze. It is covered with great apple orchards filled with soft pink blossoms in spring. As you might expect from all this, Normandy cooking features tender veal, sauces made of thick cream and golden yellow butter. It is scented with the fresh aroma of Calvados, a potent spirit distilled from apple cider. Dessert here is often a delicious apple pie. The cheese of the region is piquant.

BRITTANY

Brittany, on the other hand, is a relatively poor province. The indifferent soil is covered with a growth of tangled weeds. There are barren plains, rocky uplands and fir woods swept by strong winds that blow off the ocean.

Ever since man can remember, the Bretons have sought their livelihood from the ocean. The whole of Britanny seems to give off the odor of silver oysters and mussels, of lobsters and shrimps, of seaweed and fish. Seafood is usually eaten fresh from the fisherman's nets, prepared as simply as possible without complicated sauces and garnishings. Here you can eat fish soups and crêpes (thin

pancakes) prepared from buckwheat. Thanks to the soft humid seawind, in early spring the finest vegetables grow in Brittany's sheltered gardens. Brittany produces France's best asparagus, cauliflower and artichokes.

THE PÉRIGORD

The southwest of France is a culinary paradise. In this region of the Périgord you can go for days and days without ever encountering a bad restaurant. Every real chef seems to have a streak of genius and every housewife is a remarkably good cook. The Périgord is the land of geese. In November these geese find their destiny in large brown earthenware pots, where they remain the whole winter to age in their own fat, called "confit".

The Périgord is also the land of the fabulous truffles, sometimes called "black diamonds". These are mysterious, black, button-capped fungi which grow underground in the shade of oak trees. When these marvellous fungi ripen in November they are found by old experienced country women who walk in the open fields leading a pig on a line and carrying a basket filled with ears of corn. Pigs are mad about truffles and sniff them out with unerring accuracy from their shady beds. The pig roots for them in the ground, but just as it gets ready to bite into the delicious fungi, the old woman quickly sticks an ear of corn in its mouth and grabs the truffle for herself. She lets the truffles stand for one day in a basket with eggs, which serve the purpose of absorbing some of the penetrating odor. On the following day she sells the truffles at the market in Sarlet, where she can

Vegetable market in the Périgord.

usually get at least $40 a pound.

The Périgord is also the home of the finest pâté, made from expensive goose liver and truffles, and produces fine duck liver, turkey, veal, pork and chicken seasoned with chopped truffles and brandy. No wonder that all the European kingdoms and principalities of the 18th and 19th century wanted a cook from the Périgord!

THE PYRENEES

As we near the snow-covered chain of the Pyrenees in the south, the cooking becomes more

piquant and spicy. The Spanish and Basque temperaments are evident in the preparation of chicken and in omelets and the sausages made with tomatoes and peppers. A good Basque fish soup should be lively and pungent enough to make the hair on your head stand on end.

THE LANGUEDOC

South of the Central Massif of Auvergne, lies the Languedoc. This land was the cradle of French civilization. It produced the first distinctive French literature and music as far back as the 11th century. The glorious contribution

of this region to France's great cuisine is the "cassoulet", a stew of white beans, goose or chicken, pork, bacon and many fine herbs. The "cassoulet" has become almost a national tradition for all of France. Though it began as a humble dish, it has made its way to the Champs Elysées. The story is told that a shoemaker who lived in one of the small villages of the Languedoc called Castelnaudary, would close his shop every Thursday and put up a sign over the door which read "closed for reasons of cassoulet."

PROVENCE

Moving farther east, we come into lovely Provence, where the sun shines with the same generosity as it does in Italy. The hills give off the odor of the herbs that have been used to enrich the cooking in the area ever since people can remember: basil and thyme, marjoram and rosemary, fennel and anise. Little wonder that all these herbs find a place for themselves in any number of Provençal dishes, for example in the famous "bouillabaisse" from Marseilles, which is believed to have originated from a Greek recipe (the Greeks ruled over Marseilles in 600 B.C.), and in the leg of lamb and the chicken as well as the charcoal grilled fish, the ratatouille or any of the colorful summer vegetable dishes.

Provence is full of olive trees with knotty trunks and silver leaves. In the troubled Mediterranean world of old, olive trees were a symbol of peace since it took them twenty years to bear fruit and it only made sense to plant them in a land of peace.

Provence is also the land of garlic. The Provençals make a sauce of garlic and olive oil which they call "aioli." It may, in fact, be the oldest sauce on earth. The Phoenicians sailed the Mediterranean Sea in narrow boats many centuries before King Solomon was born. They took jars and vats of this sauce with them on their journeys and ate it with the fish they caught. The Phoenicians, like many other people around the Mediterranean) and some modern health food advocates) ascribed considerable powers to garlic. They thought it provided stamina and combated infection and disease.

THE FRENCH ALPS

From Provence's hot sun we move to the snow-covered tops of the French Alps that rise to a height of more than 14,000 feet. The economy of mountain regions is of necessity somewhat spartan. The people eat what the mountains and hills can produce, mainly potatoes and milk and cheese from the cows that graze in Alpine meadows. Not surprising, then, that the most characteristic dishes of the French Alps consist of potatoes, milk, cream and cheese. But these dishes are prepared with true French taste and feel for the right blend of ingredients. "Gratin Dauphinois" (Potatoes au Gratin Alpine Style) is a simple Alpine dish that is fit for a king!

LYON

Traveling north through the Rhône valley we arrive at Lyon, the gastronomical stronghold of France. Lyon is a city where it is impossible to eat mediocre food. Here you find the really great chefs and the famous "mères," a dedicated breed of ageing ladies who run small restaurants and do the cooking themselves.

The whole region is famous for its cooking, and in Lyon it is especially good. You can eat the best chicken in the world, prepared with a cream sauce, or eggs and truffles, or the whitest of frog legs from the swamps of Bresse, a bare 35 miles away. You can eat the best beef or the most tender ham prepared in white wine and smothered in hay, or trout out of the mountain streams of the Cévennes prepared in a sauce made from crayfish from the brooks of the neighboring Jura or pike perch fished from Lake Geneva.

BURGUNDY

Still farther north, we come into the historic province of Burgundy, where each dish is mellowed with a sauce prepared with fragrant Burgundy wine. In Burgundy almost everything is brilliantly cooked in red and white wine: not only chicken, but also eel and even eggs are poached in a wine sauce.

After a rain you can find the thick Roman snails that are such a delight to eat. The snails are cleaned and put back into their shells, which are then stuffed with a stiff sauce of butter, garlic and parsley, and baked.

This is also the land of exuberant wine festivals centered on the vaulted winecellars of historic cloisters and abbeys where people feast in the grand old style of the Middle Ages. Burgundy is an area where wine is a food, a tradition and a way of life.

ALSACE

We end our gastronomic travels through France in Alsace, the area right by the German border. Here the cooking combines the substantial quality of German food with the refinement of French cooking. You can eat the best cauliflower in the world, the finest sausages and priceless fruit pies and tarts.

The secret of great French cooking lies in two things. The first is, as it must be, the good quality of the raw materials. There are no people in the world more difficult or critical than the French when it comes to buying food. French bakers must knead fresh bread at least twice a day to satisfy the Frenchman's craving for crisp loaves tasting exactly as bread should. Even in the smallest inland villages you can get fresh fish. The French are never happier than when they can go into the country to buy fresh first quality butter, eggs, cheese, vegetables, fruit and honey.

The second part of the secret of good cooking is patience. If it concerns eating and drinking, a Frenchman is never in a hurry. He is always ready to wait for absolute perfection. He is patient enough to age cheese slowly until it reaches the perfect degree of piquancy. He is patient enough to leave the wine in the cellar until it reaches its peak. He has the patience to simmer a sauce until all the flavor and aroma have blended just enough, or to watch a meat dish slowly reach perfection over the lowest heat for hours.

This exemplary patience comes from the Frenchman's great respect for food. There is the story of an old French marquis who stood beside a basket of pears in his room. He carefully picked up each pear, tenderly examined it and then replaced it in the basket. Finally he chose just the pear he wanted and then called his butler: "Jacques," he said, "wake me up tonight at precisely twelve minutes after three. Just at that moment this pear will have reached the perfect degree of ripeness and that is the moment I should like to eat it."

Wines

In the sixteenth century there was a French king who, of all his handsome titles, preferred to be known as "King of France and Lord of the best vineyards in the world." The title may have been slightly presumptuous, but no one would argue with its accuracy.

France has the best vineyards in the world. Nowhere on earth are so many great wines produced in such a small area. The reason for this lies in a happy combination of circumstances. The French climate is predominantly cool: spring is humid, summers are moderate and the autumn is long and sunny. French soil is rocky and loose, it retains warmth but does not hold water. And not least, the French wine growers and vintners have an inborn feel for balance and harmony, they have faultless good taste and a deep love for wine.

LOIRE VALLEY

From the area around the Loire, France's most beautiful and poetic river, where the French Kings of the Renaissance built castles for their wives and mistresses, comes a group of lovely white wines and the pleasant rosés which supposedly cooled the bad temper of Josephine de Beauharnais, Napoleon's first wife.

ALSACE

In Eastern France, close by the German border in Alsace, there are vineyards that produce wines with the odor of spring blossoms. These Alsatian wines are light and fruity and are sometimes called "the young girls" by the French.

CHAMPAGNE

In the low billowing hills of the north are the Champagne vineyards. This is a delicate white wine which is bottled not more than four months after it has been pressed. It is then put in deep mile-long cellars which lie under the chalk-cliff vineyards. By a natural process, a second fermentation takes place in the wine and carbon dioxide is formed. The bottles are specially corked and reinforced with wire so that the gas cannot escape and remains in the wine. When the wire is loosened and the cork is skillfully pried off, releasing a cool flow of this festive wine, it bubbles out into the glass and you can enjoy "the smile of France" as it is called.

BURGUNDY

More than a thousand years ago, monks laid out the vineyards for Burgundy wines on the slopes of a chain of hills overlooking the eastern border of France, the Côte d'Or. They chose the spot on which to plant grapevines by tasting the soil. Obviously this method had a great deal to recommend it since the best wines of Burgundy are still those grown on the grounds chosen by the monks.

Burgundy wines are luxurious and full-bodied, they are velvety in color and may have a faint odor of violets or cinnamon, or of raspberries and blackberries. White Burgundy wines, which look slightly greenish-gold in the bottle, are dry and subtle with a distinctive bouquet and a nutty taste.

CÔTES DU RHÔNE

From the area around the Rhône, where the sun has a southern glow, comes the robust and herb-scented Côtes du Rhône, with its deep-red color. White wines are not very numerous.

Vintage along the Rhône and in the Elzas. The mule is typical for the wine regions around the Rhône, as the deep basket characterizes the Elzas vineyards.

BORDEAUX

From around the western port city of Bordeaux come the fine Bordeaux wines. There are more than 10,000 "châteaux" (small castles) in this area of gently rolling hills. Most of France's greatest wines bear the names of one of Bordeaux' seventeen districts, and of the many wines bottled in the châteaux, the best are labelled *crus classés*. The great wine districts of Bordeaux, each with its characteristic soil, surround the city like a wreath.

Médoc, one of the best known, produces a strongly flavored, light and aristocratic red wine. Graves makes a pleasant soft white wine and a robust red wine. Sauternes produces amber colored, honey-sweet white wines with a flower fragrance. Saint Emilion has full-bodied, masculine, dark red wines. Pomerol, Bourg and Blaye all have dark sparkling, full-bodied red wines.

THE CHANNEL

BELGIUM

NORD

PICARDIE

LUXEMBURG

GERMANY

NORMANDIE

ROUEN

CHAMPAGNE

LORRAINE

BRETAGNE

ANJOU

RÉGION PARISIENNE

PARIS

NANTES

ALSACE

PAYS DE LA LOIRE

CENTRE

LOIRE

BOURGOGNE

FRANCHE-COMTÉ

SWITZERLAND

ATLANTIC OCEAN

POITIERS

BERRY

POITOU CHARENTES

VIENNE

LIMOUSIN

AUVERGNE

BRESSE

SAVOIE

LYON

BORDEAUX

DORDOGNE

RHÔNE-ALPES

ITALY

AQUITAINE

MIDI-PYRÉNÉES

LANGUEDOC

PROVENCE

MARSEILLE

NICE

SPAIN

MEDITERRANEAN SEA

CORSE

WINES

Dordogne
Monbazillac
Bergerac
Parchément

Bordeaux
Médoc (Margaux,
St. Julien,
Pauillac, St. Estèphe)
Graves
Sauternes
Côtes de Bordeaux
Entre deux Mers
St. Emilion
Pomerol
Côte de Fronsac
Côte de Bourg
Côte de Blaye

Loire
Pouilly Fumé
Sancerre
Vouvray
Bourgueil
Saumur
Anjou
Muscadet

Champagne
Champagne
Bouzy

Alsace
Reisling
Sylvaner
Pinot
Gewürztraminer
Tokay
Muscat

Bourgogne
Chablis
Côte de Nuits (Nuits-
St. Georges,
Gevrey-Chambertin,
Vosne-Romanée,
Chabolle-Musigny)
Côte de Beaune
(Pommard, Volnay,
Meursault,
Puligny-Montrachet,
Aloxe-Corton)
Mâconnais
(Pouilly-Fuissé)
Châlonnais (Mercurey,
Rully, Givry)
Beaujolais (Fleurie,
Juliénas, St. Amour,
Chiroubles, Morgon,
Brouilly)

Côtes du Rhône
(Côte Rôtie,
Hermitage,

Chateauneuf-du-Pape,
Tavel, Gigondas)

Franche Comté
Arbois
Château Châlon

Provence
Côtes de Provence
Cassis

Languedoc-Rousillon
Blanquette de Limoux
Banyuls
Muscat de Frontignan

In France, wine drinking is
an art, and like any art it
has certain rules which
must be followed. There is
nothing difficult or
mysterious about how to
use wine properly for the
table. The rules to follow
are all simple and based on
common sense, but they
can add a great deal of
pleasure to wine drinking
and can make any wine
yield its best qualities.

Which wine first?

If you intend to serve
several wines during the
course of a single meal,
always drink white before
red, light before strong,
dry before sweet and
cheap before expensive.
That way you can always
get the best value from
your wine.

HOW TO DRINK

Tasting:
The art of wine-tasting is
the way to judge the
characteristics of a wine. It
calls on the three senses:
sight, smell and taste.

Sight:
The taster looks at the
wine, to examine its color
and brilliance:
– pale or dark yellow, with
golden or greenish tints,
for white wines;
– light or dark red, with
shades of color going from
ruby to garnet, for red
wines;

– various pinks for **rosé** wines, sometimes with a coppery tone. The wine will be seen best if it is held to the light, in a very clear, uncolored glass. Cut glass shows up color and brilliance.

Smell:
The taster tests the "bouquet" of the wine, which may be strong, delicate or fresh. It will be full in full-bodied, rich wines. It sometimes recalls certain fruits or flowers. The best way to smell the bouquet is to fill the glass only half-full, and roll the wine round the sides of the glass to release the scent.

Taste:
The flavor of the wine will inform the experienced taster about its origin, the nature of the soil it comes from, the vines that produced it, its age, and the methods of wine-making employed. The tongue and the palate will catch the after-taste: some wines are fruity, others flat, lacking in after-taste, harsh or full-bodied. Do not smoke while tasting wine.

Wine cellar master from Bordeaux.

"MARRYING" WINES AND FOODS

With fish, oysters, shell-fish:
dry white wines, dry white sparkling wines, brut (very dry) Champagne.

With entrées and hors-d'oeuvre:
dry or medium dry white wines, rosé wines.

With meat and poultry:
red wines, rich in bouquet and not too full-bodied.

With game:
the great red wines, full-bodied, generous and strong.

With cheeses:
great red wines, good vintages, with strong cheeses; regional white wines with mild soft cheeses.

With "foie gras":
according to preference, either red or sweet white wines from among the great names.

With the sweet course:
Champagne, other sparkling wines, sweet wines, sweet natural wines.

With fruit:
sweet white wines, Champagne, naturally sweet wines. Champagne can accompany a whole meal on its own.

WINE TEMPERATURES

– White and rosé wines are served cool, but never iced (between 44°F. and 54°F. for dry wines.) A good white wine which is too cold loses its bouquet and taste.

– Sweet wines are served even cooler.

– Sparkling wines and Champagne are served slightly chilled. Place the bottle in an ice-bucket some hours before it is drunk. Never use the freezer and never put ice in the wine, or it will lose its fizz.

– Red wines are served **chambrés**, that is at room temperature (between 59°F. and 65°F.). To achieve this, keep them for two or three days, standing upright, in the room where they are to be drunk. An exception is made for Beaujolais and other Primeur wines which should be served at cellar temperature (50°F.).

– Never heat a bottle of wine.

THE CATEGORIES OF FRENCH WINES

1. A.O.C.
2. V.D.Q.S.
3. VIN de TABLE
a) VIN de PAYS
b) VIN de TABLE

WHAT IS MEANT BY APPELLATION D'ORIGINE

The character of a wine is bound up with the place where it is produced: the soil and the subsoil, climate, situation and local vegetation, all play a part in giving the wine its own quality. If any one of these changes, the wine changes too. But these **natural** factors, although they are essential, are not the only ones involved. Man, in the person of the "vigneron", also plays a decisive role in choosing the varieties of vines, the methods of cultivation and wine-making and in deciding how to keep the wine.

The combination of these natural and human factors give the wine its own **original quality**, and is expressed by the appellation d'origine.

This is why it is necessary to describe fine wines – wines which have this original quality – by the name of the place they come from – their **appellation d'origine.**

The **appellation d'origine** may only be used for wines made according to the local practice in the place named on the label.

The category "appellation d'origine contrôlée" (A.O.C.) offers a double guarantee: ORIGIN and QUALITY. They are wines which satisfy the requirements of production as laid down by the I.N.A.O. (Institut National des Appellations d'Origine) and which were confirmed by a regulation of the Ministry of Agriculture. These conditions apply particularly to:

– The area of production.
– The types of grape varieties used.
– The pruning and cultivation methods.
– The maximum yield per hectare.
– The minimum alcoholic content before any enriching takes place.
– Methods of vinification and preservation
in other words to anything purporting to the vine and wine from its origin until it is finally sold.

WHAT ARE V.D.Q.S. WINES?

WINES OF SUPERIOR QUALITY (VINS DÉLIMITÉS DE QUALITÉ SUPÉRIEURE)

This category of wine has been defined by the law of 18th December 1949. V.D.Q.S. wines are controlled by regulations similar if somewhat less strict than A.O.C. wines. These regulations provide for the delivery of a stamp (reproduced below), given by a local viticultural syndicate when it is satisfied that the wine fulfills a number of conditions laid down by a decree of the Ministry of Agriculture bearing on the following points:

– area of production
– type of grape varieties
– minimum alcoholic content of the wine
– methods of cultivation and vinification (yield).

Over 60 regional or local appellations make up the V.D.Q.S. category and offer a complete choice of red, white and rosé wines. The production of V.D.Q.S. wines is shared by six wine producing regions:
– Lorraine,
– Central West,
– Lyonnaise and Bugey,
– Rhône Valley,
– Languedoc/Roussillon,
– South West,

For example: **Corbieres, Minervois** and **Coteaux du Languedoc** are V.D.Q.S. wines.

The V.D.Q.S. stamp is not a trade-mark. It is a guarantee by the groups of wine-makers, in accordance with strict rules, that their wine is of good quality and genuine origin.

WHAT IS A VIN DE PAYS

The category known as VINS DE PAYS was defined by a decree of 1973. It corresponds to the elite of Table Wines which have had the advantage of a geographical entity.

To obtain this denomination, VINS DE PAYS must satisfy some very strict quality criteria as mentioned below:
• They must be produced from noble grapes or recommended grapes grown in a certain territory (department, zone or village) defined in a very precise manner by the decree: they must bear the name of that area. (For example: Vin de Pays des Côteaux de Vidourle.)
• They must have a minimum natural alcoholic content of 10% for wines produced in the mediterranean zone; 9.5% or 9% for those produced in other areas.
• They must satisfy various analytical tests bearing on the limitation of the amount of sulphur dioxide or volatile acidity they contain.

• They must pass tasting tests by a Tasting Commission appointed by the Institut des Vins de Consommation Courante.

These VINS DE PAYS are good wines free from all blending, which guarantee to the consumers QUALITY, HONESTY, ORIGIN.

Contrarily to all the other wines of the VIN DE TABLE category to which they belong, the VINS DE PAYS do not have to show on their label the alcoholic content of the wine.

In their zone of production they can be given such names as COTE, COTEAU, MONT, VAL and in individual VINEYARDS MAS and DOMAINE but must **never** be designated as CHATEAU or CLOS.

Finally if their quality and good reputation justify it they may eventually be promoted into the V.D.Q.S. category.

Cheeses

A few of the 400 French cheeses.

In a moment of almost serious despair, President de Gaulle once said: "How is it possible for people to govern themselves in a land where there are more than four hundred different kinds of cheeses?"

Cheese is an important part of any hot meal in France and a Frenchman eats two hot meals each day. Cheese is served after the main course and before the dessert or fruit. Sometimes the cheese course is only a pretext for another glass of the wine that has been served with the main course. Cheese and wine make a perfect gastronomic combination: "a happy marriage" as the French say.

THE GREAT CHEESE FAMILIES

Cheeses may be classified by the milk from which they are made: cow's, goat's or ewe's milk, or they can be classified according to their origin: Normandy, Auvergne, Jura, Savoie, etc. It is more helpful, however, to group them in families according to their consistency, and in this case, cheeses belonging to the same family may be made from milk of different animal origins. (Each cheese mentioned in the text will be followed by (G) when made from goat's milk and by (E) when made from ewe's milk. All others are made using cow's milk.)

SOFT CHEESES

Accounting for more than 30% of French production, soft cheeses represent the largest family, from the tonnage point of view. They are smooth in consistency and ripen fairly quickly. They are moist and can dry out if exposed to too much ventilation, therefore special precautions must be taken to preserve them.

There are three categories:

SOFT CHEESES WITH WHITE RIND: the rind is velvety, the interior is creamy. Examples: Camembert, Brie, Carré de l'Est, Coulommiers, Valençay (G) and certain cream cheeses usually sent under brand names . . .

SOFT CHEESES WITH BRINE-WASHED RIND: they are gold in color and have a distinctive flavor. The best known are Livarot, Maroilles, Munster, Géromé, Pont l'Evêque, Reblochon . . .

SOFT CHEESES WITH NATURAL RIND: such as Sainte Maure (G) or Crottin (G). They are essentially goat's cheeses.

In general, for the overall soft-cheese family, flavor depends upon ripening: the riper the cheese, the stronger the flavor.

FRESH CHEESES form a special category which includes mainly cream and cottage cheeses which are sometimes flavored with herbs, garlic or pepper. Most of them are made from cow's milk.

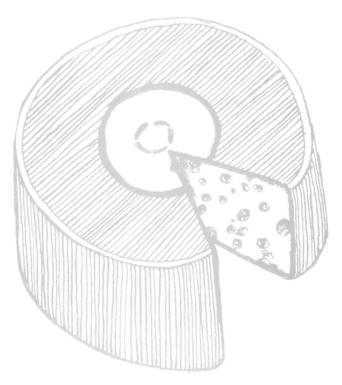

HARD CHEESES

These are produced in mountain areas. They are cooked, then pressed and come in the form of large wheel-shapes. They are easy to store and to preserve and are greatly appreciated. Most representative of this family are Emmenthal, Comté and Beaufort.

SEMI-HARD CHEESES

These cheeses are pressed but uncooked and contain very little water. The maturing process is slower and they can therefore be stored for longer periods of time than the soft and blue-veined cheeses. This family includes. Cantal, one of the oldest cheeses, as well as Saint Paulin, Tomme de Savoie, Saint Nectaire and Pyrénées cheese . . .

BLUE-VEINED CHEESES

These are unpressed, uncooked cheeses made from cow's or ewe's milk. Mold cultures are introduced into the milk and these give the cheese its blue veins. The best known and one of the oldest is Roquefort, made exclusively from ewe's milk. Bleu d'Auvergne, Bleu de Bresse and Fourme d'Ambert should also be mentioned . . . In general, these cheeses are strong-flavored, with the exception of Bleu de Bresse which has a milder taste.

PROCESSED CHEESES

They are so-called because of the manufacturing process which involves melting and blending different types of cheese, particularly pressed cheeses. This family includes: processed Gruyère cheese, cheese-spreads (in portions or "cocktail" cubes) . . . sometimes walnuts, grapes or almonds are added. These cheeses should be kept in a cool place, free from drafts. They are mild, creamy and very popular.

HISTORY

Many French cheeses have an ancient history. Take Roquefort, for example, which comes out of the barren highlands of Rouergue. In this very poor area where the ground is rocky and hardly anything grows except rye, people have been making sheep's cheese since prehistoric times.

According to legend, there was once a young shepherd who sat in one of the deep caves eating Roquefort cheese with rye bread. Evidently he went off and left some of his cheese and bread lying in the cave. Upon his return, three weeks later, he was surprised to find that the cheese now had blue-green streaks. The shepherd did not know it, but the streaks came from a mold called Penicillium (the same mold from which penicillin comes) and these streaks were produced when spores from the moldy rye came in contact with the cheese. But he did know that it tasted delicious. That was about two thousand years ago and ever since then, the inhabitants of this poor valley have left this sheep's cheese in the caves of Roquefort to ripen and produce the mold.

Soft, pungent Camembert cheese from Normandy was created around 1791 by an industrious country woman, Madame Harel. She is reputed to have received two statues and a kiss from Napoleon for her discovery.

Paris and Surroundings
Brie
Coulommiers
Saint-Paulin

Northern France and Champagne
Maroilles
Caprise des Dieux

Alsace
Carré de l'Est
Munster

Normandie
Camembert
Monsieur
Neufchâtel
Pont l'Evêque
Boursin
Demi-Suisse
Livarot

Bretagne
Port du Salut
Saint-Paulin
Le Roi

Anjou and Poitou
La Hippe
Saint-Maure
Saint-Paulin
Cremet

Berry
Valençay
Crottin
de Chavignol

Bourgogne
Epoisses

Bresse
Bresse Bleu

Franche-Comté
Gruyère
Comté

Savoie
Reblochon
Tomme de Savoie
Tomme au marc de raisin

Provence
Banon
Poivre d'Ane
Tomme d'Arles

Auvergne
Roquefort
Bleu des Causses
Cantal
Saint-Nectaire
Bleu d'Auvergne

Scallops with tomato and garlic

Coquilles St. Jacques provencale

4 servings

- 1 pound scallops
- ¼ cup all purpose flour
- 1½ tablespoons butter
- 2 medium sized tomatoes, peeled, seeded and chopped
- 2 cloves garlic, crushed
- 2 tablespoons finely chopped parsley
- ¼ teaspoon salt
  Freshly ground black pepper
  Tomato sauce

Dredge the scallops in flour. Heat the butter in a frying pan and brown scallops for three minutes over moderately high heat. Add tomatoes, garlic and parsley. Season with salt and pepper. Stir carefully and simmer over low heat for 10 minutes. Serve very hot on scallop shells or small dishes topped with tomato sauce.

Fruits of the sea in pastry

Croustade aux fruits de mer

8 servings

    2 packages frozen individual
      patty shells or 1 prepared
      pie shell
    1 egg, lightly beaten

Filling:
    1 cup dry white wine
    ½ cup water
    ½ cup clam broth (from
      canned clams)
    1 small yellow onion, cut
      into thin slices
    1 slice lemon
    1 pound flounder fillets
    ½ pound scallops
    12 medium sized shrimp
      Freshly ground black pepper
      to taste
    1 (5 ounce) can whole
      baby clams
    ¼ pound mushrooms, finely
      chopped
    1 tablespoon butter
    1 teaspoon lemon juice

Sauce:
    1½ tablespoons butter
    1½ tablespoons flour
    1 tablespoon parsley,
      finely chopped
    2 egg yolks
    ¼ cup heavy cream

Thaw the patty shells and form into 2 balls. Knead on a floured board for one minute. Roll out two circles of puff pastry, one about 12 inches in diameter and the other about 9 inches. (Cut circles using dinner plates as a guide.) Sprinkle a cookie sheet with water. Place the smaller sheet on top of the larger sheet and brush with beaten egg. Bake pastry in a 400° oven for 20 to 25 minutes until the pastry is puffed and golden, or bake a prepared pie shell and serve this dish as a one crust pie. Place the wine, water, clam broth, onion slices and lemon in a skillet. Add the fish fillets, scallops and shrimp. Bring to simmering point and poach fish for 8 minutes. Remove fish. Strain the poaching liquid into a clean saucepan and boil until 1¼ cups liquid remain. Sauté mushrooms for 5 minutes in 1 tablespoon butter and lemon juice.

To make the sauce:
Melt the butter in a small saucepan. Stir in the flour. Add the reduced poaching liquid gradually. Add parsley. Combine egg yolks and cream and add to the sauce. Remove sauce from heat and stir in mushrooms. If you are making a two crust pie, remove the top crust. Place the flounder, scallops and clams in the pastry shell. Spoon the sauce over the fish. Arrange the shrimp round the edge of the pastry. Cover with the top circle of pastry. Bake in a preheated 400° oven for 5 minutes and serve hot.

Eggs with shrimp

Oeufs au crevettes

6 servings

    6 hard boiled eggs
    3 tablespoons butter
    3 scallions, finely chopped
    1 tablespoon parsley, finely
      chopped
    ½ teaspoon tarragon
    1 cup small shrimp, chopped
      into small pieces
    1 tablespoon mild (Dijon)
      mustard
    ½ cup heavy cream
      Pinch salt
      Freshly ground black pepper
    3 tablespoons grated
      Parmesan cheese
    1 teaspoon additional butter

Chop eggs finely. Sauté shallots in hot butter. Add eggs, parsley, tarragon, shrimp, mustard and heavy cream. Season with salt and pepper. Heat mixture for 3 minutes. Place in a buttered baking dish or individual small dishes. Sprinkle with grated cheese, dot with butter and place under a preheated broiler for 3 minutes until bubbling hot and lightly browned. Serve with freshly made toast.

Fruits of the sea in pastry

Salad Riviera style

Salade Niçoise

4 servings

- 8 large lettuce leaves
  (preferably Romaine or
  Boston lettuce)
- 2 hard boiled eggs, quartered
- 2 medium sized ripe tomatoes,
  cut into wedges
- 8 canned anchovy fillets
- 8 black pitted olives, halved
- 1 (6 ounce) can tuna,
  flaked into large pieces
- 1 green pepper, cut in half
  and then into strips
- 2 teaspoons capers

For the dressing:
- 1½ tablespoons olive oil
  or vegetable oil
- 1½ teaspoons tarragon vinegar
- ½ teaspoon salt
  Freshly ground black
  pepper
- 1 clove garlic, crushed

Simmer green pepper in
boiling water for 5 minutes and
rinse in cold water. Wash the
lettuce leaves and dry with
paper towels. Place the lettuce
leaves in a salad bowl and
arrange all the remaining
ingredients on top. Combine
olive oil, vinegar, salt, pepper
and garlic. Toss the salad with
the dressing just before serving.

Salad Riviera style

In prehistoric caves discovered in France, ancient fossils of snail shells have been found alongside the fossilized remains of fish bones and oyster shells. Very good circumstantial evidence that the taste for snails must be as old as mankind itself. The ancient Romans had extensive snail farms. The Roman snail farmer Fulvius Hirpinus imported young snails from Africa and the Balkans for Roman gourmets and raised them in large earthenware pots. To enhance their flavor he fed them a steady diet of wheat flour which had been cooked in wine to make a kind of porridge. Roman cooks made a very delicious dish out of the snails with a piquant sauce of olive oil, wine, anchovies, pepper and cumin.
The best and most delicious snails of France come from the vineyards of Burgundy and Alsace. But snails are loved so much both in France and abroad

that the French vineyards cannot produce enough of them and the French have to import a large number from Turkey.
After snails are caught they are left to fast for a certain period so that they can get rid of any poisonous foods they may have eaten. They are then cooked in a little ash and water while still in their shells, removed from the shells and cooked again with garlic, onion, and preferably a dash of brandy. The shells are then very carefully washed. If the snails are not used immediately, they are canned or frozen and the shells are packed separately in bags. Snails can be bought in this way in delicatessens and gourmet food stores all over the world. They need only be heated with butter and herbs. In France, however, people prefer to cook snails fresh, and in the country people still believe that there is no better cough medicine than snail broth.

Snails in wine

Escargots à la Bourguignonne

4 servings

- ⅔ cup butter
- 3 anchovy fillets
- 2 scallions, finely chopped
- 2 tablespoons parsley,
  finely chopped
- 2 cloves garlic, crushed
- 1 tablespoon brandy or
  Pernod (opt.)
- 1 package (24) snails and
  shells
- 2 tablespoons fine bread
  crumbs
- 2 tablespoons white wine

Beat the butter with a wooden spoon until softened. Rinse anchovies in cold water to remove excess salt. Pat anchovies dry on paper towels. Mash anchovies and add to the butter. Add scallions, parsley, garlic and brandy to butter. Chill butter one hour until firm. Place a teaspoon of butter in each shell. Slip a snail into each shell and seal in place with remaining butter. Press breadcrumbs onto the butter. Place snails in snail dishes or muffin tins; or crumble aluminum foil and spread on a cookie sheet. Place shells in depressions in the foil to prevent them from tipping. Sprinkle white wine over shells. Bake in a 375° oven for 8 minutes. (If the snails are prepared in snail dishes but without shells, bake for only 5 minutes). Serve hot.

Ham quiche

Quiche au jambon

6 servings

Pastry:
1½ cups sifted all purpose flour
½ teaspoon salt
½ cup butter, cut into small
    pieces
1 egg yolk
3 tablespoons cold water

Filling:
½ pound boiled ham, cut into
    small pieces
¼ pound Swiss cheese, grated
4 eggs
1 tablespoon flour
1 cup milk
½ cup heavy cream
¼ teaspoon salt
    Freshly ground black pepper
3 tablespoons butter, melted

Sift the flour with the salt into a bowl. With a pastry blender or the fingertips, blend the butter into the flour. Stir in the egg yolk and water. Form the pastry into a ball. Wrap in wax paper and chill for 30 minutes. Knead the pastry on a lightly floured board for 2 minutes. Roll and fit the pastry into a 9 inch pie plate. Add diced ham and grated cheese to the uncooked pastry shell. Combine eggs, flour, milk, cream, salt and pepper. Pour over the ham and cheese. Add melted butter. Bake in a 400° oven for 30 minutes.

Ham quiche

Bacon and egg pie

Quiche Lorraine

6 servings

Pastry:
1¼ cups sifted all purpose flour
½ teaspoon salt
3 tablespoons butter or
    margarine, cut into small
    pieces
3 tablespoons solid shortening
3 tablespoons ice water

Filling:
½ pound bacon
¼ pound (1 cup) Swiss
    cheese, grated
4 eggs
1 tablespoon flour
1¼ cups milk or half and half
    or heavy cream
½ teaspoon salt
    Freshly ground black pepper
1 tablespoon butter, melted

Measure flour and salt into a bowl. Add butter or margarine and shortening. Combine with a pastry blender or fingertips. Add water a little at a time. Stir with a fork and form pastry in a ball. Wrap in wax paper and chill for 20 minutes. Roll on a lightly floured board and fit pastry into a nine inch pie plate.

Filling:
Fry bacon until crisp. Drain and crumble the bacon. Place in the uncooked pastry shell with grated cheese. In a small bowl combine eggs, flour, milk or cream, salt and pepper. Pour over the bacon and cheese. Add melted butter. Bake in a preheated 375° oven for 30 minutes until custard is firm and golden. Serve hot or cold.

Onion pie

Tarte à l'oignon

4 servings

Pastry:
1 cup sifted all purpose flour
¼ teaspoon salt
¼ cup butter cut into small
    pieces
1 egg
2 tablespoons cold water

Filling:
3 tablespoons butter or
    margarine
6 medium sized yellow onions,
    cut into thin rings
¼ teaspoon salt
    Freshly ground black pepper
    Dash nutmeg
3 egg yolks
⅔ cup heavy cream

Measure flour into a bowl. Add salt. Combine butter with the flour using a pastry blender or fingertips. Add egg and water. Stir with a fork, and form pastry into a ball. Wrap in wax paper and chill for one hour. Roll out the pastry and fit it into an 8 inch pie plate, flan ring or quiche tin. Fry onions in hot butter over moderate heat. Cover skillet and simmer onions for 30 minutes, stirring occasionally. Season onions with salt, pepper and nutmeg. Combine egg yolks and cream with a fork and add to the onions. Remove from the heat and fill into pastry shell. Bake in a 400° oven for 30 minutes. Serve hot.

Onion and tomato pie

Pissaladière

4 servings

Pastry:
½ *package (1¼ teaspoons)*
 dry yeast
2 *tablespoons lukewarm*
 water
1¼ *cups sifted all purpose flour*
¼ *teaspoon salt*
2 *tablespoons cold butter cut*
 into small pieces
1 *egg*

Filling:
3 *tablespoons olive oil or*
 vegetable oil
6 *medium sized onions, cut*
 into thin rings
2 *cloves garlic, crushed*
2 *medium sized tomatoes,*
 peeled, seeded and chopped
¼ *teaspoon oregano*
¼ *teaspoon salt*
 Freshly ground black pepper
1 *(2 ounce) can anchovy*
 fillets
12 *black olives, pitted*

Dissolve yeast in water and allow to stand for 10 minutes. Sift flour into a bowl. Add the salt. Blend the butter into the flour with a pastry blender or fingertips. Add egg and cold water. Stir with a fork and form into a ball. Knead lightly for one minute. Place pastry in a bowl. Cover with a towel and leave for two hours. The dough will rise slightly. Knead dough for two minutes until smooth. Roll out dough on a floured board and fit into an eight inch pie plate, flan ring or quiche pan. In the meantime, heat oil in a skillet. Add onions and garlic. Cover and simmer for 15 minutes, stirring occasionally. Add tomatoes and oregano. Season with salt and pepper and simmer uncovered for 15 more minutes until all the liquid has boiled away. Fill onions and tomatoes into the pie shell. Bake 30 minutes in a 375° oven. Decorate baked pissaladière with anchovies arranged in a criss cross design. Place halved olives in the spaces between anchovies. Serve hot.

Chicken livers flamed in brandy

Foie de poulet

6 servings

    2 tablespoons butter
  ½ yellow onion, finely chopped
    1 carrot, finely diced
    1 pound chicken livers
    3 slices boiled ham, diced
    3 mushrooms, sliced thinly
      or 1 (3 ounce) can
      mushrooms, drained
    2 tablespoons brandy (opt.)
    2 tablespoons flour
  ½ cup white wine and
  ½ cup beef broth
    1 cup seedless green grapes
    2 tablespoons finely chopped
      parsley for garnish

Heat the butter in a large skillet. Sauté the onion three minutes until transparent. Add carrot and continue cooking for 2 minutes. Add chicken livers and stir over high heat until almost tender. Add ham and mushrooms and cook two minutes. Add brandy and light it with a match immediately. When the flames have died down, stir in the flour and add wine and broth gradually, to form a medium thick sauce. Add grapes and cook just until the grapes have heated through. Garnish with parsley.

Mushrooms provençale

Champignons Cévenols

4 servings

    1 pound mushrooms
  ½ cup olive oil
  ¼ teaspoon salt
    1 small clove garlic, crushed
    1 tablespoon finely chopped
      parsley
    4 tablespoons fresh breadcrumbs

Wash the mushrooms. Separate the stems from the caps. Chop the stems finely. In a heavy skillet, heat the oil. Add the caps, cover with a circle of wax paper and cook over low heat 10 minutes. With a slotted spoon, transfer them to a plate or shallow bowl. Add the stems to the skillet, raise the heat and sauté 3 to 4 minutes. With the slotted spoon, remove the stems to a small mixing bowl and mix in the salt, garlic and parsley. Place the mixture on top of the caps. Add the breadcrumbs to the skillet and sauté until golden. Sprinkle over the mushrooms. Cover the plate and let the mushrooms stand 1 day before serving.

Artichokes vinaigrette

Artichauts vinaigrette

6 servings

    6 artichokes
  ½ lemon
    1 teaspoon salt

Vinaigrette sauce:
  ½ teaspoon salt
      Freshly ground black pepper
    1 clove garlic, crushed
  ½ teaspoon mild (Dijon)
      mustard
    2 tablespoons vinegar
    6 tablespoons light olive oil
      or salad oil
    3 tablespoons parsley,
      finely chopped
    3 tablespoons chives, finely
      chopped
    1 tablespoon capers
    1 tablespoon sweet gherkins,
      finely chopped
    1 hard boiled egg, finely
      chopped

Cut off the artichoke stems very close to the bottom. This will enable them to stand without tipping when they are served. Remove any blemished outer leaves. Snip off the point of each leaf with a pair of scissors, cutting about ¼ inch down each leaf. Plunge artichokes into a large pot of simmering salted water. Add lemon half. Cover and simmer 45 minutes or until a leaf will pull away easily. Combine the ingredients for the vinaigrette sauce in the order listed. Serve sauce in individual small containers. Serve artichokes hot or cold.

Cheese puff

Gougère

6 servings

- 1 cup milk
- 4 tablespoons butter, cut into small pieces
- ½ teaspoon salt
  Freshly ground black pepper
- 1 cup sifted all purpose flour
- 4 eggs
- 1 cup Swiss cheese, grated
- 2 tablespoons milk

Place the milk, butter, salt and pepper in a saucepan. Bring milk to boiling point adjusting the heat so the butter has completely melted when the milk boils.
Remove the pan from the heat and add the flour all at once. Stir the flour into the milk vigorously and place the pan over a moderate heat. Cook for two minutes until the dough can be formed into a ball and there is a film of flour on the bottom of the pan. Remove the pan from the heat and add the eggs one at a time beating each egg well into the mixture before adding the next egg.

Reserve ¼ cup of cheese. Beat remaining cheese into the dough. Butter and flour a cookie sheet. Draw a 9 inch circle in the flour. With a soup spoon, place balls of dough around the circle so that the balls are just touching each other. They will run together as they bake. Brush with milk and sprinkle with remaining cheese. Bake in a 375° oven for 40 minutes. Remove from the oven and cool on a wire rack before breaking into pieces.

In Burgundy this pastry is considered the ideal accompaniment to a glass of wine. It can also be served with a salad instead of bread, or the center may be filled with either meat, chicken or fish prepared in a sauce.

Eggs from the Basque

Pipérade Basquaise

4 servings

- 2½ tablespoons olive oil or vegetable oil
- 4 scallions, finely chopped
- 2 cloves garlic, crushed
- 2 green peppers, cut into strips
- 3 medium sized tomatoes, peeled, seeded and chopped
- ¼ teaspoon salt
  Freshly ground black pepper
- ¼ teaspoon thyme
- 1 bay leaf
- 3 tablespoons butter
- 4 slices Canadian bacon
- 8 eggs

Heat the oil in a skillet. Sauté scallions and garlic for two minutes. Add peppers and continue cooking for three minutes. Add tomatoes, and season with salt and pepper. Add thyme and bay leaf. Simmer uncovered for 15 minutes stirring occasionally. Fry bacon in one tablespoon butter until lightly browned on both sides. Season eggs with salt and pepper. Scramble eggs in remaining 2 tablespoons butter. Place the eggs on a hot serving plate. Make a trough down the center. Fill trough with vegetables. Arrange bacon round the sides of the dish.

Eggs from the Basque

Terrine of chicken

Terrine de poulet

8 servings

    1 pound (3 cups) cooked
      chicken, turkey or game
    1 pound sausage meat
    ½ pound sliced boiled ham,
      diced
    2 cloves garlic, crushed
    2 eggs
    1 teaspoon tarragon
    1 tablespoon parsley, finely
      chopped
    ¼ cup brandy
    ½ teaspoon salt
      Freshly ground black pepper
    ½ cup butter, softened
    ½ pound bacon, thinly sliced

Cut chicken into small pieces
and put aside. Mix together the
sausage meat, ham, garlic, eggs,
tarragon, parsley, brandy,
salt, pepper and butter. Line a
one and a half quart casserole
with three quarters of the
bacon. Top with a layer of
sausage mixture and then a
layer of chicken. Repeat until
all the ingredients are used.
Top with a layer of sausage.
Cover with remaining bacon.
Cover the casserole. Place in a
pan of hot water and bake in
a 375° oven for two hours.
Chill for at least four hours
before slicing. Serve with
freshly made toast.

Terrine of chicken

Chicken pâté

Chicken pâté

Pâté de volaille

10 servings

    1¼ pounds boneless cooked
      chicken or turkey
    ½ pound cooked pork
    ½ pound cooked ham
    2 cloves garlic, crushed
    3 scallions, finely chopped
    1 medium sized onion, finely
      chopped
    1 tablespoon parsley, finely
      chopped
    1 bay leaf
    ¼ teaspoon thyme
    ½ teaspoon salt
      Freshly ground black pepper
    2 eggs, lightly beaten
    1 tablespoon flour
    ½ cup butter, softened
    ¼ cup brandy
    ½ pound bacon

Grind or chop the chicken,
pork and ham into very small
pieces. Add garlic and scallions,
onion, parsley, bay leaf and
thyme. Season with salt and
pepper. Add eggs, flour, butter
and brandy to the meat mixture.
Stir until well combined. Line
a 1½ quart casserole with
bacon slices. Add the meat
mixture and top with remaining
bacon. Cover casserole and
place in a pan of hot water.
Bake in a 350° oven for 1 hour.
Remove pâté from the oven.
Place a weight on top of the
pâté. Refrigerate for at least
one day before slicing.

Onion soup

Soupe à l'oignon

4 servings

- 3 tablespoons butter
- 3 large onions, thinly sliced
- 1 tablespoon flour
- ½ teaspoon salt
  Freshly ground black pepper
- 5 cups beef broth
- 4 thick slices French or
  Italian bread
- 4 tablespoons grated
  Parmesan cheese
- 4 tablespoons grated Swiss
  or Gruyère cheese

In a heavy pan, melt the butter, add the sliced onions and cook slowly stirring occasionally, until golden. Sprinkle on the flour and stir for a few minutes to cook the flour. Season with salt and pepper. Add the broth, stirring constantly. Bring to a boil, lower the heat and let the soup simmer, partially covered, for 30 minutes. Toast the slices of bread in the oven until brown. Place them in a large ovenproof soup tureen or individual bowls. Preheat the broiler. Sprinkle the bread with Parmesan cheese. Pour the soup over the bread and top with the Swiss or Gruyère cheese. Brown the cheese under the broiler and serve immediately.

Onion soup is, among its other virtues, considered, a delicious remedy for a hangover after an evening of drinking. In Paris' better days the small bistros near the 'Halles', the splendid open-air market of the capital, had an early-morning clientele of partygoers in evening dress who mixed gaily with butchers and porters to share the benefits of onion soup. In those days the market was still held in the middle of the street and at night fresh fish, meat and vegetables arrived from the provinces. The bistros stayed open all night to serve wine and soup

Cream of lettuce soup

Velouté laitue

6 servings

- *3 heads Boston lettuce*
- *2 tablespoons butter*
- *1½ teaspoons salt*
- *Freshly ground black pepper*
- *4 cups water*
- *½ cup heavy cream*
- *Juice of ½ lemon*
- *6 thick slices French or Italian bread, toasted*

Wash the lettuce, remove the cores and quarter the heads. Cook in boiling, lightly salted water for 10 minutes. Drain and chop the lettuce roughly.

Melt the butter in a saucepan, add the lettuce, cover with a circle of wax paper and cook slowly for 5 minutes. Remove the paper and sprinkle lettuce with the salt and pepper; add the water and bring to a boil. Lower the heat and simmer, partially covered, for 1 hour. Purée the soup in a blender or force through a sieve. Return it to the pan, add the cream and lemon juice, and heat thoroughly before serving. Float a round of toasted bread in each bowl. You may also chill the soup for several hours and serve it cold.

Cream of lettuce soup

Fresh pea soup

Potage Saint Germain

4 servings

- *1 Boston lettuce*
- *¼ pound butter*
- *2 pounds unshelled peas or 1 package frozen peas*
- *½ teaspoon salt*
- *1 teaspoon sugar*
- *4 cups water*
- *Freshly ground black pepper*

Wash lettuce and shred leaves into strips. Melt the butter in a saucepan. Add lettuce, shelled peas, salt and sugar. Cover and simmer over low heat for 10 minutes. Add water and simmer another 10 minutes until the peas are tender. Purée the soup in a blender. Return to a clean saucepan. Add pepper. Bring soup to simmering point. Serve hot.

Potato soup

Potage Parmentier

6 servings

- *4 cups chicken broth*
- *½ teaspoon salt*
- *4 medium sized all purpose potatoes*
- *3 yellow onions, chopped*
- *3 fresh leeks, chopped or 1 additional onion*
- *½ teaspoon chervil or marjoram*
- *2 tablespoons parsley, finely chopped*
- *½ cup heavy cream*
- *1 tablespoon butter*

Bring chicken broth to simmering point and add salt. Peel potatoes and cut into eights. Add potatoes, onions and leeks to broth. Cover and simmer for 20 minutes. Mash potatoes into the broth using a potato masher to form small pieces of potato. Add chervil or marjoram, parsley and cream. Add butter and serve hot.
Note: To make vichyssoise, purée the soup in a blender adding one additional teaspoon of salt. Chill the soup for at least 4 hours. Add ½ cup more chicken broth if soup appears too thick.

Country style vegetable soup

Garbure

8 servings

4½ pounds vegetables in season
    such as: zucchini, cabbage,
    carrots, string beans, bell
    peppers, leeks, turnips,
    broccoli
1 piece cooked ham (about
    ½ pound)
1 piece lean bacon (about
    ½ pound)
½ teaspoon salt
    Freshly ground black pepper
1 bay leaf
½ teaspoon thyme
1 tablespoon chopped parsley
½ teaspoon dried marjoram
3 cloves garlic, crushed
2 ounces prosciutto or
    country ham, cut into small
    pieces
    Slices of rye bread

Clean the vegetables and cut
into rough pieces. Place the
ham and bacon, fat side up,
in a large soup pan. Add all
the vegetables (except cabbage,
if used), salt, pepper, bay leaf,
thyme, parsley, marjoram and
garlic; almost cover with
water and bring to a boil.
Lower the heat, cover the pan
and simmer 2 hours. Add the
proscuitto and cabbage, if used.
Cover and simmer another
hour. Strain the broth into a
warm soup tureen. Cut the
bacon and ham into pieces and
place the meats and vegetables
in a warm dish. In individual
soup bowls, place a slice of
rye bread, top with some of
the meat and vegetables and
pour over the hot broth.

Carrot soup

Potage crécy

4 servings

3 tablespoons butter
1 pound carrots, peeled and
    diced
1 small onion, chopped
1 medium sized potato,
    peeled and diced
½ teaspoon salt
    Freshly ground black pepper
½ teaspoon sugar
3 cups beef broth
1 tablespoon chopped parsley
1 teaspoon chopped chervil
    or marjoram

Melt the butter in a heavy
saucepan, add the carrots,
onion, and potato. Season with
the salt, pepper and sugar.
Cover and cook over low heat
for 15 minutes. Add the
broth and bring to a boil.
Lower the heat, cover and
simmer for another 15 minutes.
Purée the soup in a blender or
force it through a sieve. Serve
the soup hot, garnishing each
serving with some of the
chopped herbs.

Vegetable soup

Potage paysanne

6 servings

½ pound lean bacon, cubed
6 small breakfast sausage
    links
1 onion, finely chopped
3 medium onions, halved
2 pounds potatoes, cubed
½ pound carrots, cubed
1 teaspoon salt
    Freshly ground black pepper
5½ cups beef broth
½ pound fresh or frozen
    green peas
½ pound fresh or frozen
    green beans

In a large heavy pot, cook the
bacon until crisp and the
sausage links until brown.
Remove the sausage links and
drain on paper towels. Strain
off all the fat from the pan,
add the onions, potatoes,
carrots, salt and pepper to the
bacon and combine thoroughly.
Lower the heat, cover and
simmer for 20 minutes. Pour
in the broth; add the peas,
beans and drained sausage
links, bring to a boil, cover and
simmer 20 minutes more.
Skim the fat from the soup or
refrigerate overnight and
lift off the congealed fat. Serve
the soup hot, placing a sausage
link and an onion half in each
bowl. This soup is really a
meal in itself.

Vegetable soup

Fresh tomato soup

Potage de tomates

6 servings

   2 tablespoons butter
   1 yellow onion, finely chopped
   1 clove garlic, crushed
   5 red ripe tomatoes
   1 tablespoon tomato paste
   4 cups chicken broth
   1 bay leaf
   1 teaspoon basil
   Juice ½ lemon
½ teaspoon salt
   Freshly ground black pepper
   2 tablespoons parsley, finely chopped, for garnish

Sauté onion and garlic in hot butter for three minutes until softened. Add quartered tomatoes, tomato paste, chicken broth, bay leaf and basil. Cover and simmer for twenty minutes. Purée the soup in a blender and strain into a clean saucepan. Add lemon juice, salt and pepper. Return soup to simmering point and garnish with chopped parsley.

Soup from Alsace

Elzekaria

6 servings

   ⅓ cup lard or rendered bacon fat
   1 large onion, finely chopped
   1 medium white cabbage
   2 cloves garlic, crushed
1½ teaspoons salt
   Freshly ground black pepper
½ pound kidney beans, soaked overnight and drained
   1 tablespoon cider vinegar

Heat the lard in a heavy pan and cook the onions until brown. Wash the cabbage and chop into large pieces. When the onions are golden, add the cabbage and garlic and cook slowly for a few minutes. Sprinkle with the salt and pepper, add the beans and cover with water. Bring to a boil, lower the heat, cover and simmer for 3 hours. Just before serving add the vinegar and serve hot.

Pumpkin soup

Soupe au potiron

6 servings

   3 tablespoons butter
   1 medium onion, finely chopped
   5 cups chicken broth
   1 teaspoon salt
   Freshly ground black pepper
   1 (1 pound) can pumpkin
½ cup heavy cream

Melt the butter in a heavy saucepan and cook the onion over moderate heat until soft. Add the broth, salt and pepper and bring to a boil. Add the pumpkin, combine it thoroughly, lower the heat and simmer, covered for 45 minutes. Add the cream and heat through. Serve hot.

The garlic sauce 'aioli' was originally served to accompany the fish cooked in the bouillabaisse. Today this lively garlic sauce is also used as a dip with raw vegetables, shellfish and the like.

Garlic mayonnaise

Aioli

Makes 2 cups

- ¼ cup breadcrumbs
- 3 teaspoons tarragon or wine vinegar
- 6 cloves garlic, crushed
- ¼ teaspoon salt
- 3 egg yolks
- 1½ cups olive oil or salad oil
- 3 tablespoons boiling bottled clam juice
- 3 tablespoons lemon juice

Place breadcrumbs in the blender. Add vinegar, garlic and salt. Add egg yolks. Turn on the motor and add oil in a steady continuous drizzle of drops. (Do not add the oil too quickly or the sauce will not thicken.) Add boiling clam juice and lemon juice. Serve with fish or vegetables.

The phoenicians sailed the Mediterranean sea in narrow boats many centuries before King Solomon was born. They took jars and vats of this sauce with them on their journeys and ate it with the fish they caught. They ascribed considerable powers to garlic. They thought it provided stamina and combatted infection and disease.

Mayonnaise

Mayonaise

3 egg yolks
¼ teaspoon dry mustard
   powder
½ teaspoon salt
   Freshly ground black pepper
3 tablespoons lemon juice
   or red wine vinegar or a
   combination of the two
1½ cups olive oil or salad oil

Place the egg yolks in a bowl.
Using a hand or standard
electric mixer or a wire whisk,
beat the yolks until they are
thick and creamy. Beat in the
mustard powder, salt, pepper
and 1 tablespoon lemon juice
or vinegar. Add the oil in a
slow, steady, continuous
stream of drops, beating
constantly, until all the oil is
used and the mayonnaise is
thick. Be sure not to add the
oil too quickly or the
mayonnaise may curdle. Beat
in the remaining lemon juice
or vinegar. If the mixture
curdles, beat an egg yolk in
another bowl until it is thick
and creamy. Add the curdled
mayonnaise by droplets,
beating continuously. Continue
until you have beaten all the
curdled mayonnaise into the
fresh egg yolk.

Hollandaise sauce

Sauce Hollandaise

⅔ cup butter
3 egg yolks
⅛ teaspoon salt
   Freshly ground black pepper
2 tablespoons lemon juice

Reserve 2 tablespoons butter.
Heat the remaining butter
until very hot. Remove butter
from the heat. Beat egg yolks,
salt, pepper and 1 tablespoon
lemon juice in a small saucepan
until slightly thickened. Place
pan over moderate heat.
Add one tablespoon cold
reserved butter and cook until
butter has melted, stirring
constantly. Add second
tablespoon of reserved butter
and continue stirring until
butter has melted. Remove
the pan from the heat. Add
hot butter a little at a time,
stirring rapidly. Add remaining
tablespoon of lemon juice.

Ravigotte sauce

Sauce ravigotte

1 cup oil
¼ cup red wine vinegar
¼ teaspoon salt
   Freshly ground black pepper
2 teaspoons mild (Dijon)
   mustard
1 tablespoon capers
1 shallot or scallion, finely
   chopped
2 tablespoons combined
   finely chopped fresh herbs
   (parsley, chives, tarragon,
   chervil) or 1 tablespoon
   dried herbs
1 clove garlic, crushed
1 hard-boiled egg, finely
   chopped (opt.)

In a small bowl, combine the
oil, vinegar, salt, pepper and
mustard and beat with a wire
whisk or fork until well
blended. Add the remaining
ingredients and beat until well
combined.

French dressing

Sauce vinaigrette

¼ teaspoon salt
   Freshly ground black pepper
1 teaspoon mild (Dijon)
   mustard
2 scallions, finely chopped or
1 teaspoon onion, finely
   chopped
1 tablespoon parsley, finely
   chopped
2 tablespoons wine vinegar
6 tablespoons olive oil or
   salad oil

Combine salt, pepper, mustard,
scallions, onion, parsley and
vinegar in a bowl. Add oil
and stir until well blended.
French dressing may be used
not only for tossed green
salads but also to marinate
cold cooked vegetables such
as asparagus, broccoli,
cauliflower and peas.
It is also very good with
cold meats and fish.

Green mayonnaise

Sauce verte

Prepare mayonnaise as
directed. Beat in 3 to 4
tablespoons finely chopped
combined green herbs such as
parsley, chives, chervil,
tarragon, basil, oregano or
boiled spinach.

Mousseline sauce

Sauce mousseline

To prepare mousseline sauce,
follow the directions for
Hollandaise sauce in the
previous recipe and add ½ cup
heavy cream. Mousseline
sauce is served with
poached fish.

Béchamel sauce

Sauce Béchamel

    4 tablespoons butter
    4 level tablespoons flour
 1½ cups milk or light cream
  ⅛ teaspoon salt
     Dash nutmeg

Melt the butter and stir in the
flour. Cook over low heat for
one minute. Add milk gradually
stirring constantly. Continue
cooking over moderate heat
for two minutes until the sauce
has thickened. Season with
salt and nutmeg. White sauce
is served with vegetables
(e.g. cauliflower, squash,
broccoli and endives).

Fish broth

Bouillon de poisson

    1 pound fish trimmings
       (heads, bones, fins, etc.)
    1 slice lemon
    3 parsley stems
    1 small onion, thinly
       sliced
    1 small carrot, chopped
  ¼ teaspoon salt
    5 peppercorns
    4 fresh mushroom stems,
       chopped (optional)
  ½ cup dry white wine or
       dry vermouth
    3 cups cold water

Place all the ingredients in a
saucepan. Bring slowly to a
simmer and simmer very
slowly over low heat for 45
minutes. Strain and cool.

White chicken broth

Bouillon blanc de volaille

 1–2 pounds chicken backs,
       necks, wings, hearts,
       gizzards
    1 large onion, washed but
       unskinned, and quartered
    1 carrot, roughly cut
    2 stalks celery, roughly cut
    1 tomato quartered
    2 bay leaves
  ½ teaspoon thyme
  10 peppercorns
    3 parsley stalks
    2 quarts water

Place all the ingredients in a
large pot and bring to a boil.
Lower the heat, partially cover
the pot and let simmer very
slowly for 3 hours. Strain the
broth. Chill it in the
refrigerator and lift off the
fat before using the broth.

Mornay sauce

Sauce Mornay

To prepare Mornay sauce,
follow the directions for
Béchamel sauce in the **above**
recipe and add ½ cup grated
Swiss cheese. Mornay sauce
is served with eggs, vegetables
and pasta such as macaroni.

Classic brown sauce

Sauce Espagnole

 2⅓ cups brown broth,
       or 3 beef bouillon
       cubes dissolved in 2⅓ cups
       boiling water
  ⅔ cup dry red wine
    3 tablespoons butter
    3 tablespoons flour
    1 teaspoon tomato paste

Place the broth and wine in a
saucepan and boil until
reduced to 1½ cups. In another
heavy saucepan, melt the
butter and add the flour.
Stir with a wire whisk and cook
for 3 to 4 minutes or until the
flour is light brown. Add the
bouillon/wine mixture
gradually, beating with a wire
whisk. Return the sauce to
the simmer and cook until
thick. Beat in the tomato paste.
Brown sauce is used to
accompany braised meats,
game and steaks.

White beef broth

Bouillon blanc de veau

1–2 pounds veal bones with
meat attached, the same
herbs, vegetables and liquid
used for white chicken broth.
Follow the directions given for
white chicken broth, **above**.

Brown broth

Bouillon brun

 1–2 pounds beef or veal
       (or both) bones with
       meat attached
    1 large onion, washed but
       unskinned, and quartered
    1 carrot, roughly cut
    2 stalks celery, roughly cut
    1 tomato, quartered
    2 bay leaves
  ½ teaspoon thyme
  10 peppercorns
    3 parsley stalks
    2 quarts water

Place the bones with meat in a
roasting pan and brown for
15 minutes in a 400° oven.
Add the vegetables and
continue browning for 10
minutes. Transfer the bones,
meat and vegetables to a large
pot, add the herbs and water
and bring to a boil. Reduce
the heat, partially cover the pot
and simmer very slowly for 4
to 5 hours. Only an occasional
bubble should break the
surface. Strain the broth, chill
it in the refrigerator and lift
off the fat before using
the broth.

Madeira sauce

Sauce Madère

Prepare Sauce Espagnole and
add 2 tablespoons Madeira.
Just before serving, beat in 1
tablespoon butter.

Velouté sauce

Sauce velouté

- 2 tablespoons butter
- 4 level tablespoons flour
- 1½ cups chicken broth
- 1 egg yolk
- 1 teaspoon lemon juice
- ⅛ teaspoon salt
  Freshly ground black pepper

Melt the butter and stir in the flour. Cook over low heat for one minute. Add chicken broth gradually, stirring with a whisk. Simmer one minute until the sauce has thickened. Add egg yolk, lemon juice salt and pepper. Velouté sauce may also be made with fish stock, (or ¾ cup clam broth combined with ¾ water) if the sauce is to be served with fish. Beef broth can be substituted for chicken broth for beef dishes.

Béarnaise sauce

Sauce Béarnaise

- ¼ cup white wine
- ¼ cup tarragon or wine vinegar
- 1 teaspoon dried tarragon
- 2 tablespoons scallions, finely chopped
- ⅔ cup butter
- 3 egg yolks
- ⅛ teaspoon salt
  Freshly ground black pepper
- ½ teaspoon dried tarragon

Place wine, wine vinegar, tarragon and scallions in a saucepan. Boil uncovered until the liquid is reduced to 2 tablespoons. Strain and reserve liquid. Reserve 2 tablespoons of butter. Heat the remaining butter until very hot. Remove butter from the heat. Beat egg yolks in a small saucepan until slightly thickened. Add strained wine and vinegar. Place pan over moderate heat. Add one tablespoon cold reserved butter and cook until butter has melted, stirring constantly. Add second tablespoon of reserved butter and continue stirring until butter has melted. Remove the pan from the heat. Add hot butter a little at a time, stirring rapidly. Season sauce with salt, pepper and tarragon. Béarnaise sauce is served with broiled steaks and fish.

Mackerel mariners' style

Maquereaux marinés au vin blanc

6 servings

   3 *pounds mackerel or*
   6 *(¾ pound) trout*
   2 *cups bottled clam juice*
   2 *cups water*
   1 *medium sized onion,*
    finely chopped
   3 *carrots, diced*
   1 *teaspoon olive oil or salad oil*
   1 *onion, cut into rings*
   2 *carrots, thinly sliced*
¼ *teaspoon salt*
    Freshly ground black pepper
   1 *lemon, sliced*
   1 *cup dry white wine*
   1 *tablespoon vinegar*
   3 *tablespoons olive oil or*
    salad oil
¼ *teaspoon thyme*
   1 *bay leaf*
   3 *sprigs parsley*
   2 *cloves*

Pour clam juice and water into a saucepan. Add onion and carrots. Cover and simmer for 30 minutes and strain. Oil a baking dish or fish poacher. Cover the bottom with half of the onion rings and thinly sliced carrots. Place the mackerel in the dish, season with salt and pepper and cover with remaining onion and carrot. Add lemon slices. Pour in the wine, vinegar, olive oil and strained **clam juice. Add the thyme,** bay leaf, parsley and cloves. Cover and poach the fish over low heat for 8–10 minutes. Remove bay leaf and parsley sprigs. Allow the fish to cool completely before serving.

PIKE

The great French connoisseur, writer and epicure of the table, Brillat Savarin, wrote that 'fish is the most inexhaustible source of culinary inspiration there is'. French cooks have always known how to use this source of inspiration very well. It is extraordinary what the French can do with the simplest and cheapest fish. To begin with, the French demand fish that is very fresh and go out of their way to obtain it. Very early in the morning at one of Paris' main stations you can see cooks from the small fish restaurants arrive to meet the trains coming from Brittany. There they personally take charge of the baskets of fresh fish from the Breton ports so that they can get it to their kitchens immediately.

King Louis XV is supposed to have awarded a prize of 9,000 gold francs for an absolutely fresh gilthead, and the absence of fresh fish was once the direct cause of a dramatic suicide: In 1671 the Prince of Condé planned a feast for King Louis XIV and some 3,000 other distinguished guests. When the fresh fish failed to arrive in time, the butler, Vatel, felt himself so disgraced that he stabbed himself with his sword.

Appropriately enough, the most famous fish restaurant in the world is Prunier in Paris. In the basement kitchen, chef Charles Verdilhac stands like a magician behind an enormous stove in which a coal fire roars and glows (the great French cooks still cook on coal stoves and will have nothing to do with electricity and gas!). Although one might imagine that the formidable chef saves his best efforts for expensive fish such as lobster,

sole and turbot, the master runs a democratic kitchen and prepares simple whiting, cod and mussels with the same care that he reserves for the more aristocratic species of the water kingdom. According to tradition, Parisian connoisseurs dine at Prunier twice a year: once early in autumn, when the chestnut trees along the wide boulevards turn yellow, to taste the oysters, and once in April, when the first young leaves of the same chestnut trees appear, to eat fresh caviar from the Gironde accompanied by a fine, soft sparkling champagne to celebrate the beginning of spring.

There is an old French saying that fish without wine is poison, and another that says 'Fish must swim three times, once in water, then in butter, and finally in wine'. All of which confirms the classical gastronomic rule that fish and wine are inseparable. A corollary of the same rule is that fish is normally accompanied by a dry white wine. The only exception to the rule is fish prepared in a very rich sauce, with which a demi-sec white wine is drunk. A refinement of the rule is that the more delicate the fish the better the wine has to be. A fine white wine is always drunk cool – but never chilled. In fact, anything ice cold that passes over the tongue deadens the taste buds to the subtleties of the meal. A good white wine should therefore never be cooler than cellar temperature (about 50°–54°). Only sweet or simple, cheap white wines are served chilled, and even then not to the point of being ice cold.

Trout with almonds

Truites aux amandes

4 servings

    4 (¾ pound) whole trout, cleaned
    1 cup milk
  ½ cup flour seasoned with ½ teaspoon salt
      Freshly ground black pepper
  ½ pound butter
  ⅓ cup sliced almonds
      Parsley for garnish
    1 lemon, cut into wedges

Dry trout with paper towels. Dip in milk and then in flour. Heat ¾ of the butter in a large skillet. Fry trout four minutes on each side over moderate heat until golden brown. Sprinkle fish with salt and pepper and keep hot. In a small skillet, heat remaining butter and brown the almonds. Place trout on a hot platter. Pour the butter and almonds over the trout. Garnish with parsley and lemon wedges.

Fish balls in Nantua sauce

Quenelles de brochet Nantua

8 servings

 1 pound package frozen
   perch fillets, skinned and
   boned
 ½ cup butter, creamed
 1 teaspoon salt
   Dash of white pepper
 1 cup water
 ¼ cup butter, cut in pieces
 1 teaspoon salt
 1 cup flour
 3 eggs
 ¼ cup butter, creamed
 ¼ cup cooked rock lobster,
   finely chopped
 2 cups Béchamel sauce,
   (page 35)

Dry the perch fillets very thoroughly on paper towels. Put them through the finest blade of a meat grinder and beat into the creamed butter along with the salt and white pepper until very well combined. In a heavy saucepan, bring the water, butter and salt to a boil. (Do not allow the water to boil before the butter melts). Add the flour all at once and beat over medium heat with a spatula until the mixture forms a ball and leaves a slight film on the bottom of the pan. Cool the paste, then add it to the perch mixture, beating vigorously. Add the eggs, one at a time, combining each thoroughly before adding another. Cover the mixture and chill for several hours. In a large pan, bring about 3 inches of water barely to the simmer. Roll the fish paste into small ovals and drop them into the water. Poach for 15 to 20 minutes making sure the water is barely simmering. Remove the quenelles with a slotted spoon and drain on paper towels. While the quenelles are poaching, beat the lobster into the ¼ cup of creamed butter. Heat the Béchamel sauce and beat in the lobster butter. Cook for 2 or 3 minutes and taste for seasoning. Place the quenelles in a serving dish and cover with the lobster sauce.

Deviled salmon

Saumon diable

4 servings

 1½ pounds salmon steaks
 ½ cup butter, softened
 1 tablespoon mild (Dijon)
   mustard
 1 tablespoon lemon juice
   Dash cayenne pepper
 2 tablespoons parsley, finely
   chopped
 1½ tablespoons vegetable oil
 ¼ teaspoon salt
   Freshly ground black pepper

Beat butter with mustard, lemon juice, cayenne pepper and parsley. Place in the refrigerator to harden. Brush salmon with oil and season with salt and pepper. Broil 4 minutes on each side. Top hot salmon with a pat of cold flavored butter. Serve hot.

Halibut with Mornay Sauce

Barbue Mornay

6 servings

 3 pounds halibut steaks
 2 cups water
 ½ teaspoon salt
 2 tablespoons lemon juice
 2 tablespoons butter
 2 tablespoons flour
 2 cups milk
 ¼ cup Swiss cheese, grated
 ¼ cup Parmesan cheese,
   grated
 ¼ teaspoon salt
   Freshly ground black pepper
 1 teaspoon mild (Dijon)
   mustard
 ½ cup breadcrumbs

Place fish in a large skillet and cover with water. Add salt and lemon juice. Simmer uncovered for 15 minutes until fish is white and flakes easily. Drain fish and keep it warm. Melt the butter in a saucepan. Stir in the flour and add the milk gradually. Add cheeses and season the sauce with salt, pepper and mustard. Place fish in a baking dish. Cover with sauce and top with breadcrumbs. Bake 5 minutes in a 400° oven until sauce is lightly browned and bubbling.

Sole Normandy style

Sole à la Normande

4 servings

16 *mussels, fresh or canned*
½ *pound mushrooms, washed,
    trimmed and quartered
    if large*
4 *tablespoons water
    Juice of one lemon*
3 *tablespoons butter*
1 *teaspoon salt*
½ *pound shrimp, cooked,
    shelled and deveined*
2 *prepackaged frozen patty
    shells, thawed*
2 *cups fish broth, shrimp
    cooking liquid or 2 chicken
    bouillon cubes, dissolved
    in 2 cups water*
4 *fillets of sole, about 1½
    pounds, folded in half*
2½ *tablespoons flour*
2 *egg yolks*
⅓ *cup heavy cream
    Sprigs of parsley*
1 *black truffle, thinly
    sliced (optional)*

If using fresh mussels, clean
as described in the recipe for
moules marinière, (page 47).
Steam in ½ cup water until
the shells open. Discard shells
and wrap mussels in aluminum
foil. In a saucepan, combine
the mushrooms, water, lemon,
juice, 1 tablespoon butter
and salt. Cover with a circle
of wax paper and cook over
low heat for about 7 minutes.
Drain and reserve the liquid.
Wrap mushrooms in aluminum
foil. Wrap the shrimp in foil.
Roll out the thawed patty shells
to make 1 sheet of dough
about ⅛″ thick. Cut 12 small

crescent shapes and bake
according to package directions.
Combine the mushroom
cooking liquid with the
bouillon in a shallow pan.
Add the fillets, cover with a
piece of buttered wax paper
cut to fit the pan and bring to
a simmer on top of the stove.
Transfer to a 400° oven and
cook 5 minutes. Do not
over-cook. Carefully, transfer
the fillets to a warmed serving
dish. Turn the oven off and
place the mussels, mushrooms
and shrimp in their foil
packages and the baked
crescent pastries, uncovered,
in the oven to reheat. Over
high heat, reduce the fish
cooking liquid to 1 cup. In a
small, heavy saucepan, melt
the remaining 2 tablespoons
butter. Add the flour and
cook 1 or 2 minutes. Beat in
the reduced cooking liquid,
stirring constantly, and bring
to a simmer. Beat the egg
yolks into the cream and
add to the sauce. Do not allow
it to boil but just heat through.
Season with drops of lemon
juice and salt and pepper if
needed. Pour the sauce over
the fillets and garnish the dish
with the mussels, mushrooms,
shrimp, crescent shaped
pastries and parsley. Place
sliced truffles on the fillets.
Serve hot.

MUSSEL

Fillet of sole Bercy

Sole Bercy

4 servings

1¾ *pounds sole or flounder
    fillets with skin removed*
½ *teaspoon salt
    Freshly ground black pepper*
3 *scallions, finely chopped*
2 *tablespoons parsley,
    finely chopped*
½ *cup white wine*
2 *tablespoons butter*

Season fish with salt and
pepper. Butter a large oval
baking dish. Add the scallions
and parsley. Add wine and
place the dish in a 350° oven
for 5 minutes. Take the dish
out of the oven. Arrange
fillets in a single layer in the
dish, top with pats of butter.
Cover the fish with aluminum
foil. Place in the oven for 15
minutes. Remove paper.
Drain off the poaching liquid.
Place under the broiler for
2 minutes. Serve hot.

Frog legs

Grenouilles

4 servings

24 *frog legs*
½ *cup milk*
½ *cup flour, seasoned with
    ½ teaspoon salt
    Freshly ground black pepper*
3 *tablespoons butter*
3 *cloves garlic, crushed*
2 *tablespoons white vermouth*
2 *hard boiled eggs, chopped*
2 *tablespoons parsley, finely
    chopped*
1 *teaspoon capers (optional)*
2 *tablespoons lemon juice*

Dip frog legs in milk and then
in seasoned flour. Shake off
excess flour. Sauté frog legs
and garlic in butter for ten
minutes until lightly browned.
Transfer frog legs to a hot
serving dish. Add vermouth
to the skillet and stir in eggs,
parsley, capers and lemon
juice. Pour all these hot
ingredients over the frog legs.
Serve hot.

Sole Normandy style

Fillet of sole au gratin in cider sauce

Sole Deauvilloise

4 servings

- ¼ *cup butter*
- ½ *pound onions, chopped*
- ½ *cup heavy cream*
- 1½–2 *pounds fillets of sole or one large flounder, head and tail intact*
- 1¼ *cups fish broth or 1 chicken bouillon cube dissolved in 1¼ cups water*
- ¾ *cup apple cider or juice*
- ½ *teaspoon salt*
    Freshly ground black pepper
    Peel of one lemon
- 1½ *tablespoons butter*
- 2 *tablespoons flour*
    Dash of nutmeg
- 1 *teaspoon dry mustard*
    Drops of lemon juice
- 3–4 *tablespoons fine dry breadcrumbs*

In a small saucepan, heat the butter, add the onions and cook until soft. Purée the mixture in the blender with 2 tablespoons of cream or force through a sieve. Place the fillets, folded in half, or the whole fish in a shallow, lightly buttered flame proof serving dish. Combine the broth, cider, salt, pepper and lemon peel and bring to a simmer. Simmer 10 minutes and strain onto the fish. Cover the fish with a buttered piece of wax paper cut to fit the pan. Bring the liquid to a simmer on top of the stove, place in a 400° oven and poach for 5 to 10 minutes. The whole fish will require the longer time.

Strain off the poaching liquid and reserve. Melt 1 tablespoon butter, add the flour and cook for a few minutes over medium heat. Add 1¼ cups of the poaching liquid, stirring constantly until smooth. Add the puréed onions, remaining cream, nutmeg, mustard and a few drops of lemon juice. Bring to a boil, stirring, and simmer a few minutes. Pour the sauce over the fish, sprinkle with breadcrumbs, dot with butter and place under the broiler for about 2 minutes or until golden. Garnish with parsley and serve hot.

Riviera mullet

Rougets aux fines herbes

4 servings

- 2 *pounds mullet*
- ¼ *cup butter*
    Sprigs of parsley
- 3 *shallots or scallions, finely chopped*
- ¼ *teaspoon dried thyme*
- 1 *bay leaf*
- ¼ *teaspoon fennel seed*
- 1 *carrot, grated*
- 1 *lemon, thinly sliced*
- 8 *black olives, chopped*
- ¼ *teaspoon salt*
    Freshly ground black pepper
- 2 *teaspoons lemon juice*
- ½ *cup dry sherry*
- 2 *tablespoons fine dry bread crumbs*
- 1 *tablespoon butter*
- 2 *tablespoons finely chopped parsley*

Clean the fish and dry thoroughly with paper towels. Melt the butter in an ovenproof dish large enough to hold the fish and add the parsley, shallots, thyme, bay leaf, fennel, carrot, lemon slices and olives. Season the fish inside and out with salt and pepper. Place in the dish, sprinkle with lemon juice and pour the sherry over all. Cover tightly with aluminum foil and bake in a 375° oven for 25 minutes or until done. Sprinkle the fish with bread crumbs, dot with butter and place under the broiler until the bread crumbs are golden. Sprinkle with parsley and serve hot.

Mackerel with fennel

Maquereaux au fenouil

6 servings

- 3 (1½ pound) mackerel
- ¾ cup butter, softened
- 6 scallions, finely chopped
- 2 tablespoons lemon juice
- 2 tablespoons fresh fennel, or dill weed or
- 1 teaspoon fennel seeds or dill seeds
- 1½ tablespoons olive oil or vegetable oil
- 1 teaspoon salt
  Freshly ground black pepper
- 6 cherry tomatoes

Sauce:
- ¼ cup dry white wine
- 4 scallions, finely chopped
- 2 egg yolks
- ½ cup hot butter
  Fennel, dill or parsley for garnish

Dry fish inside and out with paper towels. Combine butter, scallions, lemon juice and fennel. Stuff the fish with this mixture. Sew or skewer the edges together. Brush the fish with oil and sprinkle with salt and pepper. Place under the broiler for ten minutes on each side. Continue cooking for ten minutes in a 400° oven. During the last five minutes add the whole tomatoes. In the meantime, prepare the sauce. Pour the wine into a small saucepan. Add the scallions and simmer over low heat for three minutes until scallions are softened and almost all the wine has boiled away. Remove the pan from the heat. Beat the egg yolks into the wine. Place the pan over very low heat. Beat in the hot butter stirring constantly. Remove the pan from the heat as soon as the sauce is thickened. Season the sauce with salt and pepper. Remove skewers from the fish and place on a hot platter. Garnish platter with tomatoes, fresh fennel, dill or parsley. Serve hot. Serve the sauce separately.

Fish soup from Marseilles

Bouillabaisse

6 servings

- 3 pounds assorted salt water fish (cod, haddock, red snapper, sea bass, etc.)
- 2 cups bottled clam broth
- 2 cups water
- 1 onion, chopped
- 2 carrots, chopped
- 2 stalks celery, chopped
- 2 stalks parsley
- 3 tablespoons olive oil or vegetable oil
- 1 onion, finely chopped
- 2 cloves garlic, crushed
- 3 medium sized tomatoes, peeled, seeded and chopped or 1 (1 pound) can tomatoes, drained and chopped
- 1 bay leaf
- 1 teaspoon fennel seeds, crushed
- ⅛ teaspoon saffron, soaked in 1 tablespoon hot water for 5 minutes
  Peel from ½ orange, finely chopped
- ½ teaspoon salt
  Freshly ground black pepper

Remove skin and bones from the fish. Cut fish into 2 inch slices and lay to one side. Put clam broth, water, 1 onion, carrots, celery and parsley in a large saucepan. Cover and simmer for 30 minutes. Strain the broth and discard the vegetables. Fry fish in hot oil, three minutes on each side, until lightly browned. Transfer fish to the broth. In the same skillet sauté onion and garlic for two minutes until softened. Add tomatoes, bay leaf, fennel, saffron with its soaking water, and orange peel. Season with salt and pepper. Simmer these ingredients uncovered for 5 minutes. Transfer to the broth with the fish. Bring broth to simmering point. Ladle into soup bowls and serve with French bread.

Mackerel with fennel

Whiting in wine sauce

Merlan au vin rouge

4 servings

> 2 tablespoons olive oil
> 1 medium onion, finely
>   chopped
> 1 tablespoon flour
> 1 cup dry red wine
> 1 cup water
> ¾ teaspoon salt
>   Freshly ground black pepper
> 2 cloves garlic, crushed
> ¼ teaspoon thyme
> 1 bay leaf
> 1 tablespoon chopped parsley
> 2 teaspoons tomato paste
> 2 large whiting, cut into 1"
>   thick slices
> 1 cup flour seasoned with
>   ½ teaspoon salt
>   Freshly ground black pepper
> 3 tablespoons olive oil
> 1 tablespoon capers

Heat the olive oil in a heavy saucepan and sauté the onion until golden. Add the flour, stir and cook for 1 minute. Pour on the wine and water, stirring vigorously. Bring to a boil and add salt, pepper, garlic, thyme, bay leaf, parsley and tomato paste. Lower the heat and simmer until the sauce is reduced to about 1¼ cups. While the sauce is reducing, dredge the fish slices in seasoned flour. Heat the olive oil until it sizzles and sauté the fish on both sides until done and golden. Drain on paper towels and place on a warmed serving platter. When the sauce is ready, remove the bay leaf, stir in the capers and pour over the fish.

Fried smelts

Buissons d'éperlans

4 servings

> 1½ pounds smelts or fresh
>   sardines
> 1 cup milk
> 1 cup flour
>   Oil for deep frying
>   Salt
>   Sprigs of parsley
> 2 lemons, thinly sliced

Clean the smelts and dry thoroughly on paper towels. Heat the oil to 375° or until almost smoking. Dip the smelts into the milk, then the flour and fry a few at a time, until golden brown. As they are done, remove and drain on paper towels. Sprinkle with salt and keep warm. When all are done, transfer to a heated bowl, mounding them slightly. Fry sprigs of parsley, drain and garnish the smelts with the parsley and lemon slices.

Poached bass

Bar poché

6 servings

> 1 (4 pound) whole bass,
>   cleaned
> 3 tablespoons lemon juice
> ½ teaspoon salt
>   Freshly ground black pepper
> ½ teaspoon either chervil,
>   tarragon or dill
> 2 tablespoons butter, melted
> 2 cups milk
> ½ onion, sliced
> ½ carrot, chopped
> 1 stalk celery, chopped
> 1 bay leaf
> ½ teaspoon peppercorns
> 2 tablespoons butter
> 2 tablespoons flour
> 2 tablespoons parsley,
>   finely chopped

Season fish inside and on the surface with lemon juice, salt, pepper and chervil. Add half of the butter inside the fish and brush skin with the remaining butter. Place fish in a baking dish. Pour in the milk and add onion, carrot, celery, bay leaf and peppercorns. Cover with foil and bake 25 minutes in a 350° oven. Remove the fish and keep it warm. Strain milk. Melt remaining 2 tablespoons butter in a saucepan. Stir in the flour and add the milk gradually. Spoon the sauce over the fish and garnish with parsley.

Fried smelts

Stuffed trout

Truite farcie

4 servings

- 4 *(1 pound) trout*
- ¾ *cups fresh breadcrumbs*
- ½ *pound mushrooms, finely chopped*
- 1 *tablespoon finely chopped parsley*
- 4 *shallots or scallions, finely chopped*
- 1 *teaspoon salt*
  Freshly ground black pepper
- ½ *cup butter*
- ¾ *cup heavy cream*
- ¾ *cup dry white wine*
- 2 *medium tomatoes, peeled, seeded and chopped*
- ½ *teaspoon salt*
- ¼ *teaspoon thyme*
- ¼ *teaspoon basil*

Clean the trout, leaving the heads intact. Combine the breadcrumbs, mushrooms, parsley, 2 shallots, salt and pepper. In a heavy pan, melt 2 tablespoons of the butter and sauté the mixture until it is fairly dry. Add ¼ cup of the cream and cook a few minutes more. Dry the trout well with paper towels and stuff them with the breadcrumb mixture. Melt the remaining butter in an ovenproof serving dish, add the trout, baste with the butter and scatter the remaining chopped shallots over the fish. Cover the pan tightly with aluminum foil and bake in a 325° oven for 15 minutes. While the trout are baking, combine the remaining cream and wine in a small pan.

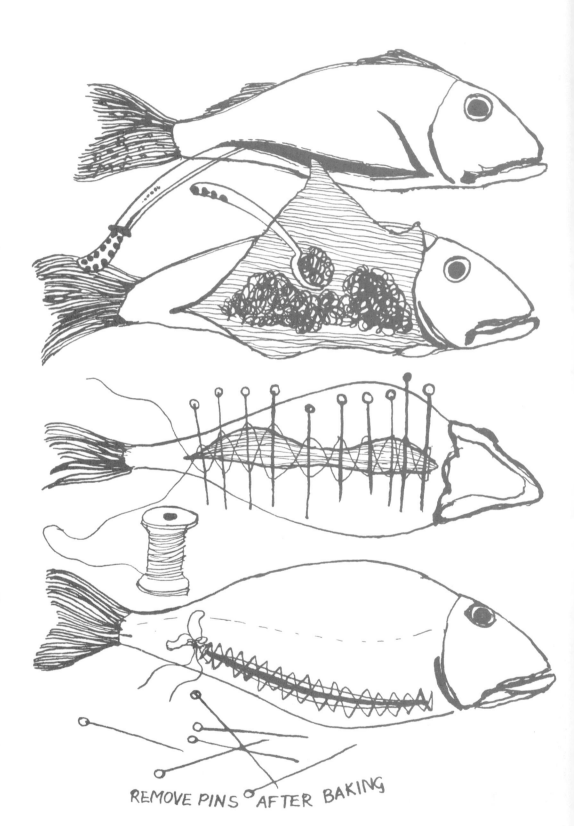

REMOVE PINS AFTER BAKING

Stuffed striped mullet

Rougets farcis aux échalotes

3 servings

- 3 (one pound) striped
  mullets or other small salt
  water fish, cleaned
- ¼ pound bacon, fried until
  crisp, and drained
- 6 scallions, finely chopped
- 3 teaspoons butter, melted
- ¼ teaspoon salt
  Freshly ground black pepper

Sauce:
- 2 tablespoons butter
- 2 tablespoons flour
- 2 cups milk
- 1 tablespoon tomato paste
- ¼ cup heavy cream
- 1 bunch parsley, finely
  chopped
  boiled small potatoes

Crumble the bacon, combine
with the scallions and stuff the
mullets. Butter three pieces
of aluminum foil and place
mullets on the foil. Sprinkle
with salt and pepper and fold
foil into little packets.
Bake in a 350° oven for 20
minutes. In the meantime,
heat 2 tablespoons butter in a
small saucepan. Stir in the
flour and add the milk
gradually. Stir in the tomato
paste and cream. Season with
salt and pepper. Simmer
sauce, uncovered over low heat
for ten minutes and then keep
it warm. Take fish out of the
packets and broil for 3
minutes on each side. Sprinkle
parsley over a platter. Place
mullets on top of the parsley
and arrange the hot boiled
potatoes on the platter.
Serve the sauce separately.

Shrimp with tarragon

Crevettes à l'estragon

4 servings

- 2 tablespoons butter
- 4 scallions, finely chopped
- 2 cloves garlic, crushed
- 2 green peppers, finely
  chopped
- 1½ pounds shrimp, shelled
  and deveined
- 2 medium sized tomatoes,
  peeled, seeded and chopped
- ½ teaspoon tarragon
- 2 tablespoons lemon juice
- ¼ teaspoon salt
  Freshly ground black pepper
- ⅓ cup white vermouth
- ½ cup white wine
- 1 tablespoon cornstarch,
  dissolved in 2 tablespoons
  cold water
- 2 tablespoons parsley,
  finely chopped

Cut the shrimp through the
back but keep the tail attached.
Heat the butter in a skillet.
Sauté scallions, garlic and
green pepper 3 minutes until
softened. Add shrimp and
cook over high heat for 3
minutes. Add tomatoes,
tarragon, lemon juice, salt and
pepper, vermouth and wine.
Simmer 5 minutes. Stir in
cornstarch dissolved in cold
water. Garnish with parsley
and serve hot on a bed of rice.

Shrimp in cream

Crevettes à la crème

4 servings

- 4 tablespoons butter
- 1½ pounds small shrimp,
  cleaned, shelled and
  deveined
- ¼ teaspoon salt
  Freshly ground black pepper
- 1 tablespoon paprika
- ⅓ cup sherry or Madeira
  wine
- ¼ cup white wine
- 1 cup heavy cream

Heat the butter in a skillet.
Add shrimp. Season with
salt, pepper and paprika and
sauté over high heat for 5
minutes. Remove shrimp to
a hot platter and keep warm.
Add sherry or Madeira and
white wine to the skillet.
Boil over high heat until only
about 4 tablespoons liquid
remain. Add cream and
continue cooking over high
heat until the cream has
thickened into a sauce.
Pour sauce over the shrimp
and serve hot. This dish is also
excellent made with 2 (12
ounce) packages frozen
langoustes or 1½ pounds
freshly boiled lobster meat.

Stuffed striped mullet

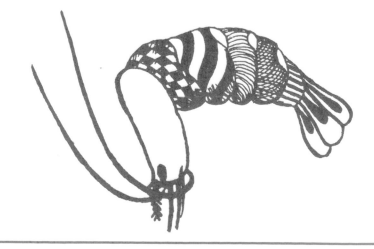

Fish soup

Cotriade

6 servings

> 3 pounds fish: such as a
> combination of sea bass,
> mullet, haddock, mackerel,
> devil fish, whiting, sardine
> 2 tablespoons olive oil
> 2 large onions, chopped
> 6 cups fish broth (see page
> 35) or 3 chicken bouillon
> cubes dissolved in 6 cups
> water
> 2 teaspoons salt
> Freshly ground black pepper
> 1 tablespoon parsley, finely
> chopped
> ¼ teaspoon dried sage
> ¼ teaspoon marjoram
> ¼ teaspoon dried thyme
> 1 bay leaf
> 1 pound potatoes cut into
> large cubes
> French or Italian bread

Clean the fish and cut into
thick slices. In a large pan,
heat the oil, add the onions
and sauté over medium heat
until brown. Add the broth
and bring to a boil over high
heat. Add the salt, pepper,
parsley, sage, marjoram,
thyme and bay leaf and simmer
3 minutes. Add the potatoes,
cover and cook over medium
heat 5 to 7 minutes. Add the
fish slices, lower the heat and
cook, covered, for 7 to 10
minutes or until the fish
flakes easily. Place fish on a
warm platter and surround
with the potatoes. Place thick
slices of bread in individual
soup bowls and pour over
the bouillon.

MACKEREL HADDOCK

Crab salad

Salade de tourteau

6 servings

- 2 pounds crabmeat, cleaned
- 6 mushrooms, sliced
- 2 tablespoons lemon juice
- 6 tablespoons olive oil or vegetable oil
- ¼ teaspoon salt
  Freshly ground black pepper
- 4 hard boiled eggs
- 2 tomatoes, cut into wedges
- 2 green peppers, cut into strips
- 12 black olives, pitted
- ¼ cup English walnuts, chopped
- 2 tablespoons parsley, finely chopped

Combine crabmeat and mushrooms in a bowl. Stir together the lemon juice, oil, salt and pepper. Moisten crabmeat and mushrooms with 2 tablespoons lemon juice and oil. Place crabmeat in the center of a serving dish. Cut eggs into wedges and arrange around the crabmeat. Place tomatoes in a bowl. Simmer green pepper strips for four minutes in boiling water. Drain and rinse in cold water. Add green pepper and olives to tomatoes. Toss with remaining lemon juice and oil. Drain and arrange around crabmeat. Sprinkle crabmeat with walnuts and parsley.

Mussels mariners' style

Moules marinière

6–8 servings

- 6–8 dozen mussels, fresh or canned with shells, if available
- 2 tablespoons butter
- 1 stalk celery, chopped
- 1 medium leek or three scallions, sliced thinly
- 1 carrot, chopped
- ¼ cup chopped parsley
- 1 bay leaf
  Coarsley ground black pepper
- 1½ cups dry white wine

If using fresh mussels, scrub the shells with a stiff brush, cleaning them well. Remove the beards with a sharp knife, rinse under cold running water, and soak in cold water for 10 to 15 minutes to remove excess sand. Discard any mussels that are open. In a large pot, melt the butter and cook the celery, leek or scallion and carrot until soft. Add the remaining ingredients and bring to a simmer. Rinse the mussels and add to the pot. Cover and steam the mussels, shaking the pan occasionally, until the shells open—about 5 to 10 minutes. Cook for 5 minutes if using canned mussels. Remove the mussels to a large warm bowl. Continue simmering the liquid for three minutes more and strain into the bowl over the mussels. Serve hot with French bread.

Poached salmon

Saumon poché

4 servings

- 1 cup dry white wine
- 2 cups water
- 1 medium onion, sliced
- 2 carrots, sliced
- ¾ teaspoon salt
- 1 bay leaf
- 4 salmon steaks
  Watercress
  Hollandaise sauce (page 34)

Place the wine, water, onion, carrots, salt and bay leaf in a heavy saucepan. Bring to a boil, lower the heat and simmer 45 minutes. Place the salmon in a lightly buttered shallow pan, strain on the liquid and cover with buttered wax paper cut to fit the pan. Bring the liquid to a simmer on top of the stove, place in a 375° oven and poach for 10–15 minutes depending on the thickness of the steaks. Drain the fish and place on a serving platter. Garnish with watercress and serve warm with Hollandaise sauce.

Mussels mariners' style

Fish fillets with capers

Poissons aux câpres

4 servings

>   2 pounds salt water fish
>   fillets: e.g. haddock,
>   cod, etc.
>   2 cups fish broth or 2 chicken
>   bouillon cubes dissolved
>   in 2 cups water
> ½ cup butter
>   Juice of 1 lemon
> ½ cup capers
>   2 teaspoons red wine vinegar
>   1 tablespoon chopped parsley

Place the fillets in a lightly
buttered flameproof dish, pour
on the broth and cover with
buttered wax paper, cut to
fit the pan. Bring to a simmer
on top of the stove. Place in
a 375° oven and poach for
10–12 minutes or until the fish
flakes easily. While the fish
cooks, melt the butter in a
small pan, stir in the lemon
juice, capers, and vinegar and
heat until bubbling. When the
fish is done, drain it and
place on a warmed serving
dish. Pour the butter over and
garnish with chopped parsley.

Fish fillets with capers

*In France, anything that has to do
with good eating and drinking is
taken so seriously that gourmets
and gastronomical writers can
deliberate endlessly over the
origin, composition and proper
name of a particular dish. One
recipe still debated by the
epicures is 'Lobster à
l'Armoricaine'.
This delicious dish of warm
lobster in a piquant sauce of
brandy, shallot, garlic, and herbs
belongs to the top of the list of
every great French cook – and
almost every one of them has
thought up his own small
variation. As a result, 'Lobster à
l'Armoricaine' is never eaten in
quite the same way in any two
restaurants.
The general concensus, at any
rate, is that the dish was
discovered in 1853 by a Parisian
restaurant owner and that it is
based on the traditional way of
preparing shellfish in the south of
France. No one knows the precise
name that was given to the recipe
at the time, though some say that
it was 'Lobster à l'Américaine' in
honor of some American guests at
the restaurant. The more
accepted view, however, is that
the name 'Lobster à
l'Armoricaine' originates from
the word 'Armorica', the old
Celtic name for Brittany, a
region that still produces
delicious lobster. The variant
name 'Américaine', it would then
appear, came much later when
American tourists in Paris
became so fond of this delicious dish.*

Breton style lobster

Homard à l'Armoricaine

6 servings

>   3 (1½ pound) live lobsters
>   or frozen lobster tails
>   3 tablespoons butter,
>   softened
>   1 tablespoon olive oil
>   1 tablespoon butter
>   1 small onion, finely chopped
>   2 scallions, finely chopped
>   1 clove garlic, crushed
>   3 tablespoons brandy, warmed
> 1½ tablespoons flour
>   2 medium sized tomatoes,
>   peeled, seeded and chopped
>   1 tablespoon tomato paste
>   2 tablespoons parsley,
>   finely chopped
>   1 teaspoon tarragon
> ¼ cup bottled clam juice
> ¼ cup water
> ½ cup white wine
> ¼ teaspoon salt
>   Freshly ground black pepper

Pierce live lobsters with a
sharp knife at the point where
the body meets the tail. Remove
uncooked lobster meat. Reserve
red coral and green tomalley
and combine with softened
butter. Keep this mixture to
one side. Cut lobster, or
partially thawed lobster tails,
into bite sized pieces. Heat oil
and 1 tablespoon butter in a
heavy skillet. Sauté onion,
scallions and garlic for two
minutes. Add lobster and cook
over moderately high heat for
3 minutes. Add warmed
brandy and light with a match.
When the flames die down
fold in the flour. Add tomatoes,
tomato paste, parsley and
tarragon. Stir in clam juice,
water and wine. Season with
salt and pepper. Cover skillet
and simmer for 15 minutes.
Stir in reserved coral butter
mixture. Simmer 2 more
minutes until the sauce has
thickened. Serve hot.

Beef Wellington

Filet de boeuf en croûte

8 servings

    5 pound fillet of beef with
       its covering fat
    1 teaspoon salt
       Freshly ground black pepper
    2 tablespoons butter
    2 pounds mushrooms, finely
       chopped
    6 tablespoons scallions,
       finely chopped
    2 tablespoons flour
    1 tablespoon lemon juice
  1/3 cup sherry or Madeira wine
    1 (3 ounce) can liver pâté
    2 packages individual frozen
       patty shells or double
       recipe for pastry (page 89)
       or 1 package pie crust mix
    1 egg yolk
    2 tablespoons milk

Have the butcher remove the
fat and tie the beef with string
at 2 inch intervals. Place the
beef on a roasting rack, cover
with the reserved fat and roast
in a 400° oven for 20 minutes.
Discard the fat. Season beef
with salt and pepper. Allow
beef to cool. It will stiffen as
it cools. Heat the butter in a
skillet and simmer mushrooms
and scallions for 15 minutes.
Stir in the flour. Add lemon
juice, and sherry. Add liver
pâté. Spread mushroom
mixture over the cool beef.
Thaw frozen patty shells.
Form pastry into a ball and
roll into a rectangle on a
lightly floured board, or prepare
alternative pastry. The pastry
should be large enough to
enclose the beef completely.

Wrap beef in the pastry sheet
folding the edges neatly. Place
beef on a buttered and floured
baking sheet. Prick the surface
of the pastry to allow the steam
to escape as the cooking is
completed. Brush pastry with
combined egg yolk and milk.
Place in a 400° oven for 15
minutes. Lower the heat to 350°
and continue cooking for 20
minutes until beef is rare and
pastry is browned. Allow the
beef to rest 15 minutes before
cutting into thick slices.
Serve hot with Madeira sauce
(page 35).
Note: There are four separate
processes in preparing beef
Wellington. The beef has a
preliminary roasting; the
mushroom mixture is prepared,
and the pastry is made. Finally,
it is all assembled and cooked.
Except for the final cooking
the other steps can be taken
over a period of two days.
This is a dramatic and
expensive dish but worthy to
serve for a very special occasion.

Pepper steak

Steak au poivre

4 servings

    4 boneless tenderloin or
       sirloin steaks
    2 tablespoons oil
 1 1/2 tablespoons peppercorns or
       1 tablespoon cracked pepper
    4 tablespoons butter
    2 shallots or scallions,
       finely chopped
  1/3 cup dry white wine
  1/4 cup beef broth
  1/3 cup brandy

Dry the steaks well with paper
towels. Rub them on both
sides with 1 tablespoon oil.
Crush the peppercorns and
press firmly into both sides
of the steaks. Let stand 1 to 2
hours. In a heavy pan, heat the
remaining oil and 2 tablespoons
of the butter until very hot.
Sauté the steaks over high heat
for about 3 minutes on each
side for rare meat. Transfer
them to a hot platter and
sprinkle with salt. Add the

shallots to the pan and saute
for a few minutes. Pour in the
wine and broth and boil rapidly,
scraping up the meat juices
clinging to the pan. Warm the
brandy, ignite it and add to the
pan. When the flames have
died down, remove the pan
from the heat and beat in the
remaining butter. Pour the
sauce over the steaks and serve.

Beef Wellington

Roast beef with garden vegetables

Boeuf bouquetière

8 servings

  6 *pound rolled rib roast*
  2 *cloves garlic, slivered*
  1 *teaspoon salt*
    Freshly ground black pepper
  1 *cauliflower*
  2 *pounds green beans*
  1 *pound asparagus*
  1 *pound new potatoes*
 ¼ *cup butter*
  8 *small tomatoes*
  8 *medium sized mushroom*
    caps
  2 *tablespoons butter*
 ¼ *teaspoon salt*
    Freshly ground black pepper
  1 *bunch watercress, washed*
    and thoroughly dried

Make slits in the roast and insert garlic slivers. **Season.**

Place the meat in a roasting pan and cook uncovered in a 450° oven for 15 to 20 minutes or until nicely browned. Reduce the heat to 350°, insert a meat thermometer and roast, basting occasionally with the pan drippings, until the meat reaches the desired degree of doneness. The total time will be 20 minutes per pound for medium rare.
In the meantime, prepare the vegetables, dividing the cauliflower into sections. Cook the cauliflower, green beans, and asparagus separately in boiling salted water until tender but still firm. If frozen vegetables are used, follow the package directions. Canned vegetables should simply be heated through. Boil the potatoes, covered, until not quite done, then sauté in the butter until golden. Blanch the whole tomatoes in boiling water for 2 to 3 minutes, making sure they remain firm. Remove the cores and slip off the skins. Sauté the mushroom caps in 2 tablespoons butter for 3 to 5 minutes and season with salt and pepper. When the roast is done, place on a warmed platter and surround with the vegetables. Garnish with watercress and serve.

Beef braised in wine

Boeuf à la mode

8 servings

  8 *carrots, sliced thinly*
  1 *onion, chopped finely*
  1 *bay leaf*
 ½ *teaspoon thyme*
  3 *sprigs parsley*
 ¼ *teaspoon salt*
    Freshly ground black pepper
  3 *pounds top sirloin or*
    eye round roast
 1½ *cups red wine*
  2 *tablespoons olive oil*
    or vegetable oil
  3 *onions, finely chopped*
  4 *cloves garlic*
 12 *large mushrooms, finely*
    chopped
  1 *teaspoon lemon juice*
 ½ *pound bacon*
 ½ *cup beef broth*
  3 *tablespoons flour*

Place carrots, onion, bay leaf, thyme and parsley, salt and pepper in a bowl. Add the beef and wine. Cover and marinate the beef in the refrigerator for 24 hours. Turn the beef every 8 hours. Remove the meat. Dry on paper towels. Strain and reserve the marinade. Heat the oil in a heavy casserole and brown the meat on all sides over high heat. Lower the heat and fry onions and garlic in the same oil for 3 minutes. Add mushrooms and lemon juice and continue cooking for 5 minutes. In the meantime, fry bacon until almost crisp. Drain and leave to one side. Heat reserved marinade with beef broth. Stir flour into onions and mushrooms. Add bacon. Replace beef in the casserole and stir in warm wine and broth. Cover and cook 2½ hours in a 350° oven.

Roast beef with garden vegetables

Beef Bourguignon

Boeuf à la Bourguignonne

6 servings

    3 pounds lean boneless
       chuck, cubed
    1 large onion, thinly sliced
  ½ teaspoon thyme
    1 bay leaf
    1 tablespoon chopped parsley
    1 clove garlic, crushed
  ½ teaspoon salt
       Freshly ground black pepper
    1 cup dry red wine
    2 tablespoons olive oil
  ¼ pound lean salt pork
       or sliced bacon, cut into
       thin strips
  18 small white onions
    2 tablespoons flour
1½ cups beef broth or bouillon
  ½ pound mushrooms
    2 tablespoons butter

Place the meat, onion, thyme, bay leaf, parsley, garlic, salt and pepper in a bowl. Combine the wine and olive oil, pour over the beef and marinate for 4 or more hours, stirring occasionally. Place the salt pork or bacon strips in a heavy casserole and sauté until the fat is rendered. Add the small white onions and sauté until tender and browned and the salt pork or bacon is crisp. Remove from the pan. Dry the cubes of beef well with paper towels and reserve the marinade. Sauté the beef in the hot fat, browning well on all sides. Sprinkle on the flour, cook for a few minutes and pour on the marinade and beef bouillon. Bring to a simmer, cover and cook for 2 hours or until beef is tender. In the meantime, lightly sauté the mushrooms in the butter. When the beef is done, taste for seasoning, add the salt pork or bacon, onions and mushrooms to the casserole and simmer another 15 minutes to blend the flavors. Serve from the casserole. This dish is best prepared one day before it is to be served.

Beef stew

Pot au feu

6–8 servings

    3 pound piece of beef (sirloin,
       bottom round, rump, etc.)
    2 marrow bones (optional)
    1 teaspoon salt
  10 peppercorns
  ½ teaspoon thyme
    1 bay leaf
    1 tablespoon chopped parsley
    2 medium onions
    4 cloves
    2 stalks celery, sliced
  ½ pound carrots, sliced
  ½ pound turnips, cubed
    2 leeks or 6 scallions, sliced
  ½ pound potatoes, cubed
    1 small cabbage, roughly cut
  ½ cup red wine
       Pickles
       Mild (Dijon) mustard
       Coarse sea salt

Place the beef, marrow bones, salt, peppercorns, thyme, bay leaf and parsley in a heavy pan. Almost cover with water, bring to a boil and skim. Reduce the heat, partially cover and simmer for 2 to 2½ hours, skimming occasionally. Spike one of the onions with the cloves and slice the other. Add these to the pot along with the celery, carrots, turnips, leeks and potatoes. Simmer, partially covered, another hour. Add the cabbage and continue simmering for ½ hour. Remove the meat and vegetables from the broth. Slice the meat and place on a platter with the vegetables. Spoon the optional marrow over slices of French bread and discard the bones. Skim any fat from the broth, add the wine and transfer to a warm bowl. Serve the meat and vegetables from the platter and pass the broth, French bread, pickles, mustard and sea salt separately.

Beef stew

Rib steak in Bordelaise sauce

Côte de boeuf à la Bordelaise

6 servings

3½ pounds rib steak with the
  bone or 2½ pounds
  boneless sirloin steak cut
  1 inch thick
2 tablespoons butter
1 tablespoon olive oil or
  vegetable oil
½ teaspoon salt
  Freshly ground black pepper
4 tablespoons finely chopped
  scallions
1 clove garlic, crushed
½ cup red wine
¼ teaspoon thyme
1 tablespoon lemon juice
1 tablespoon brandy
4 tablespoons butter, softened
2 tablespoons finely chopped
  parsley
2 tablespoons beef marrow,
  (diced and simmered in
  boiling water for 3 minutes),
  if available

Sauté steak in a heavy skillet
in combined, hot butter and oil.
Adjust the heat to prevent the
butter from burning. Cook
steaks 4 to 5 minutes on each
side. Transfer to a hot plate.
Season with salt and pepper
and keep hot. Stir scallions
and garlic into the same
skillet. Sauté scallions for
three minutes. Add wine,
stirring in all the browned
juices from the bottom of the
pan. Add thyme, lemon juice
and brandy. Boil over high
heat until the wine is reduced
to about 3 tablespoons.
Remove skillet from the heat
and beat in the butter and
finely chopped parsley.
Add beef marrow if available.
Serve sauce separately.

Veal kidneys with tomatoes

Rognons de veau aux tomates

4 servings

1½ pounds calves' or lamb
  kidneys
1 onion, finely chopped
2 tablespoons butter
8 button mushrooms
1 teaspoon paprika
1 tablespoon mild (Dijon)
  mustard
1½ tablespoons flour
1 cup beef broth
2 tomatoes, peeled, seeded
  and chopped
¼ cup heavy cream
¼ teaspoon salt
  Freshly ground black pepper
2 tablespoons parsley,
  finely chopped

Cut kidneys into small pieces,
cutting around white inner core.
Sauté onion in butter for 3
minutes until softened. Add
and sauté kidneys and
mushrooms for 3 minutes
over high heat. Lower the heat
and stir in paprika, mustard
and flour. Add beef broth,
tomatoes and cream. Season
with salt and pepper. Simmer
5 minutes until kidneys are
tender. Garnish with finely
chopped parsley.

Veal stew

Blanquette de veau

6 servings

2½ pounds stewing veal cut
  from the shoulder and cut
  into 2 inch squares
1 onion, chopped
2 carrots, sliced
½ teaspoon salt
1 bay leaf
3 stalks parsley
2 cups water
3 tablespoons butter
4 tablespoons scallions,
  finely chopped
6 mushrooms, quartered
3 tablespoons flour
2 egg yolks
⅓ cup heavy cream
2 tablespoons finely chopped
  parsley

Place veal, onion, carrots, salt,
bay leaf and parsley in a
casserole. Add cold water and
heat to simmering point.
Simmer five minutes. Remove
scum which rises to the surface.
Cover casserole and simmer
over low heat for 1½ hours.
Sauté scallions in 2 tablespoons
butter in a skillet. Add and
brown the mushrooms.
Transfer to the casserole.
Add remaining tablespoon of
butter to the same skillet.
Stir in flour and add ¾ cup
hot liquid from the casserole.
Stir to form a sauce.*
Combine egg yolks and cream
and add to the sauce. (Do not
allow the sauce to boil or the
egg yolks will curdle). Stir
sauce into the casserole.
Allow to thicken. Garnish
with parsley. Serve hot.

*May be prepared in advance
to this point.

Rib steak in Bordelaise sauce

Steak in red wine

Entrecôte marchand de vin

4 servings

 4 fillet mignon steaks
   (6–8 ounces each, cut
   1½ inches thick)
 1 tablespoon butter
 1 tablespoon vegetable oil
 ½ teaspoon salt
   Freshly ground black pepper
 ¾ cup red wine
 4 tablespoons scallions,
   chopped
 ½ teaspoon thyme
 1 bay leaf
 ¼ teaspoon Bovril
 3 tablespoons butter, softened

Sauté steaks in hot butter and
oil over high heat for 3 minutes
on each side. Place on a hot
serving dish. Season with salt
and pepper and keep warm.
In the meantime, prepare the
sauce: Pour the wine into a
small saucepan. Add scallions,
thyme and bay leaf. Boil over
high heat until reduced to ½
cup. Stir in Bovril (meat glaze)
and butter. Boil 2 more
minutes. Remove the bay leaf.
Pour sauce over steaks and
serve immediately.

Beef with mushrooms

Boeuf aux champignons

4 servings

 2 pounds fillet of beef
 1 tablespoon butter
 1 tablespoon olive oil or
   vegetable oil
 1 onion, finely chopped
 1 clove garlic, crushed
 4 mushrooms, thinly sliced
 2 tablespoons flour
 1 teaspoon tomato paste
 ½ cup red wine
 ¾ cup beef broth
 ½ teaspoon salt
   Freshly ground black pepper
 ½ teaspoon thyme
 2 tablespoons parsley,
   finely chopped

Cut beef into thin slices and
then into strips. Sauté beef
strips in a skillet in combined
butter and oil over high heat
for 5 minutes. Stir beef to
prevent it from sticking. Stir
in onion and garlic. Cook 3
minutes. Add mushrooms and
cook 2 minutes. Fold in flour
and tomato paste. Stir in wine
and beef broth. Season with
salt and pepper. Add thyme
and simmer 3 more minutes.
Garnish with parsley. Serve hot.

Beef casserole

Estouffade de boeuf

8 servings

 ½ pound lean sliced bacon
 3½ pounds bottom round of
   beef, cubed
 ½ cup all purpose flour
   seasoned with ¼ teaspoon
   salt
   Freshly ground pepper
 2 shallots or green onions,
   sliced
 2 medium sized onions,
   roughly cut
 2 large carrots, thickly sliced
 2 cups dry red wine
 ¼ cup brandy
 2 cloves garlic, crushed
 ½ teaspoon thyme
 1 bay leaf, crumbled
 1 tablespoon finely chopped
   parsley
 ½ teaspoon salt
   Freshly ground pepper
 1 tablespoon tomato paste
 ½–1 cup beef broth

Simmer the bacon in water
for 10 minutes to render the

fat. Drain, reserve 3 slices and
roughly chop the remainder.
In a heavy flameproof casserole
just large enough to hold the
ingredients, lay the 3 bacon
strips on the bottom. Roll the
beef cubes in seasoned flour
and place half of them close
together in a layer on top of
the bacon. Cover the beef
with half of the vegetables and
chopped bacon. Repeat the
layers with the remaining
beef, vegetables and bacon.
Warm the wine in a small pan.
Add the brandy, garlic, thyme,
bay leaf, parsley, salt, pepper
and tomato paste. Combine
thoroughly and pour into the
casserole. Use beef broth as
needed to almost cover the
contents of the pan. Bring to a
simmer on top of the stove.
Cover with aluminum foil and
then a lid and place in a 300°
oven for 3 hours. Skim off the
fat, taste for seasoning and
serve from the casserole.

Beef casserole

Veal cutlets with mushrooms

Côte de veau Vallée d'Auge

4 servings

 4 veal cutlets, 4 ounces each,
   pounded thin
 2 tablespoons butter
¼ pound mushrooms, thinly
   sliced
¼ pound small white onions,
   blanched in boiling salted
   water for about 8 minutes
   or until tender
¾ cup heavy cream
½ teaspoon salt
   Freshly ground black pepper
¼ cup apple brandy
 1 teaspoon lemon juice
 1 tablespoon cornstarch
   dissolved in 2 tablespoons
   water

In a heavy skillet, heat the
butter until foaming and sauté
the cutlets for about 2 minutes
on each side. Transfer them
to a warm serving plate.
Add the mushrooms and onions
to the skillet and sauté 3
minutes until softened. Pour
on the cream. Season with salt
and pepper and simmer 3
minutes. Add the apple brandy
and simmer another 3 minutes.
Add lemon juice to taste and
thicken into a sauce with the
cornstarch mixture. Pour the
sauce over the veal and
serve hot.

Veal Riviera style

Veau à la Niçoise

6 servings

2½ pounds boneless veal roast
 2 cloves garlic, quartered
½ teaspoon salt
   Freshly ground black pepper
 3 tablespoons olive oil or
   vegetable oil
 3 medium sized onions, sliced
 3 large ripe tomatoes, peeled,
   seeded and chopped
 1 tablespoon finely chopped
   parsley
½ teaspoon marjoram

Make deep slits in the veal and
insert garlic quarters. Brown
meat lightly in hot oil. Remove
meat from the pan. Add onions
and simmer over medium heat
for 3 minutes. Add tomatoes,
parsley and marjoram.
Season veal with salt and
pepper. Place veal on the bed
of vegetables. Roast in a 300°
oven for 1½ hours. Slice and
serve hot or cold.

Calves liver with grapes

Foie de veau Véronique

6 servings

 6 slices calves' liver
½ cup flour seasoned with
   ½ teaspoon salt
   Freshly ground black pepper
 1 tablespoon oil
 2 tablespoons butter
¼ cup sweet vermouth
 1 cup beef broth
¼ teaspoon thyme
½ cup white seedless grapes

Dredge the liver slices in the
seasoned flour. Melt the butter
and oil in a large skillet.
When the butter is foaming,
sauté the liver slices for 2
or 3 minutes on each side.
Remove to a heated platter.
Add the vermouth, broth and
thyme to the skillet. Boil over
high heat, scraping up the
browned bits clinging to the
bottom of the pan. When the
sauce has reduced to about
¾ cup, add the grapes and
heat through. Taste for
seasoning. Pour the sauce over
the liver and serve hot.

Pork chops in apple cider

Côtelettes de porc au cidre

4 servings

 4 thick pork chops
 1 tablespoon butter
 1 tablespoon olive oil or
   vegetable oil
½ teaspoon salt
   Freshly ground black pepper
 2 tablespoons flour
1¼ cups apple cider
 1 clove garlic, crushed
 1 teaspoon rosemary
 1 teaspoon capers

Brown chops in combined hot
butter and oil. Cook chops
6 minutes on each side. Remove
chops from the skillet and
season with salt and pepper.
Discard all but 2 tablespoons
fat from the skillet. Stir flour
into the skillet. Add apple
cider, garlic and rosemary.
Simmer sauce 5 minutes until
thickened and slightly reduced.
Replace chops. Cover and
simmer for 15 minutes. Stir
capers into the sauce 5 minutes
before serving time. Serve hot.

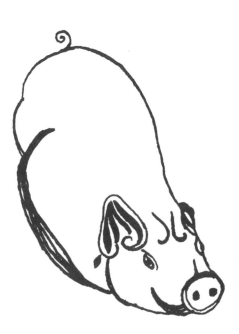

Ham in parsley and wine sauce

Jambon persillé

3 pounds cooked ham, cut in large cubes
½ teaspoon thyme
1 bay leaf
½ teaspoon salt (more or less depending on saltiness of the ham)
Freshly ground black pepper
2 shallots or scallions, finely chopped
1 stalk celery, chopped
2½ cups chicken broth
2½ cups dry white wine
½ to ¾ cup finely chopped parsley
2 packages unflavored gelatin
½ cup water
1 to 2 tablespoons tarragon vinegar

In a large pan, place the ham, thyme, bay leaf, salt, pepper, shallots, celery, broth and white wine. Bring to a simmer, cover and cook slowly 30 minutes. Remove the ham with a slotted spoon and place in a wet serving bowl. Toss the ham with a little of the chopped parsley. Sprinkle the gelatin over the water to soften. Strain the liquid in which the ham has cooked into another pan. Add the softened gelatin and stir to dissolve, then add the vinegar and remaining parsley. Cool until the liquid starts to set and pour over the ham. Refrigerate overnight before serving.

Sauerkraut Alsatian style

Choucroute Alsacienne

8 servings

3 pounds sauerkraut
½ teaspoon caraway seeds (optional)
1 tablespoon black peppercorns
2 cups white wine
½ pound bacon, thickly sliced
4 pork sausages
4 bratwurst or knackwurst
4 frankfurters
8 pork chops
¼ teaspoon salt
Freshly ground black pepper
1 pound smoked or cooked ham, cut into small pieces
2 pounds potatoes, boiled

Rinse sauerkraut under cold running water and squeeze dry. Place sauerkraut in a large skillet. Add caraway seeds, peppercorns and white wine. Cover and simmer 20 minutes. Fry bacon until crisp and all the fat has rendered. Drain bacon and reserve bacon fat. Return 1 tablespoon fat to the skillet. Brown pork sausages, bratwurst and frankfurters in hot fat. Drain on paper towels. Add two more tablespoons reserved bacon fat to the skillet. Brown pork chops in hot fat for 8 minutes. Turn, season with salt and pepper and cook 8 minutes on the second side. Brown ham in the same skillet. Arrange pork chops , **ham and** sausage on a bed of sauerkraut. Place in a 375° oven for ten minutes. Serve hot with boiled potatoes.

Sauerkraut Alsatian style

Pork loin with prunes

Noisettes de porc aux pruneaux

4 servings

1 cup dried prunes
1 cup red wine
1½ pounds pork loin, cut into thick slices or 4 thick pork chops
1 tablespoon butter
1 tablespoon olive oil or vegetable oil
½ teaspoon salt
Freshly ground black pepper
2 tablespoons flour
½ cup beef broth
1 tablespoon red currant jelly
½ cup heavy cream
2 tablespoons finely chopped parsley

Soak prunes in red wine for 12 hours. Simmer prunes and wine, uncovered, in a small saucepan for 30 minutes until prunes are tender and the wine has reduced slightly. Brown pork chops in combined hot butter and oil. Continue cooking 6 minutes on each side. Remove chops and season with salt and pepper. Discard all but 2 tablespoons of fat in the skillet. Stir in flour. Add beef broth and wine from the prunes. Keep prunes warm. Add red currant jelly and cream. Simmer sauce five minutes. Return chops to the skillet and simmer 15 minutes over low heat. Garnish with warm prunes and chopped parsley.

Pork and lamb baked with potatoes

Beckenoff

6 servings

- 2 tablespoons butter
- 6 Idaho potatoes, peeled and sliced thinly
- 2 large onions, sliced thinly
- 1 teaspoon salt
  Freshly ground black pepper
- 1½ pounds pork tenderloin, trimmed and sliced thinly
- 1½ pounds lamb shoulder, trimmed and sliced thinly
- ½ teaspoon thyme
- 1 bay leaf
- 4 tablespoons finely chopped parsley
- ½ cup white wine
- ½ cup chicken broth
- 1 tablespoon cornstarch dissolved in 2 tablespoons cold water
- 1 tablespoon butter
- 2 tablespoons finely chopped parsley

Butter a large baking dish with 1 tablespoon of butter. Cover with half of the potatoes, then arrange half of the onion rings on top of the potatoes. Season lightly with salt and pepper. Place half of both kinds of meat on top of the onions. Season with salt and pepper. Add thyme, bay leaf and half of the parsley. Add remaining meats and season again with salt and pepper. Add a layer of onion rings, a layer of potatoes and again season with salt and pepper. Pour in wine and chicken broth. Dot with remaining tablespoon of butter.

Cover tightly with aluminum foil. Bake in a 350° oven for 2 hours. Remove foil, stir in cornstarch paste and heat until sauce is thickened. Dot surface with butter. Brown potatoes under the broiler for 3 minutes. Garnish with finely chopped parsley and serve hot.

Broiled lamb chops in onion sauce

Côtelettes de mouton Comtoise

4 servings

- 8 loin lamb chops
- 2 tablespoons olive oil or vegetable oil
- ½ teaspoon salt
  Freshly ground black pepper
- 8 medium sized onions, sliced
- 2 cloves garlic, crushed
- 2 tablespoons butter
- 2 tablespoons flour
- ⅓ cup heavy cream

Heat butter and simmer onions and garlic over moderate heat for 30 minutes until a soft purée is formed. Stir in flour and add cream. Simmer another 15 minutes. Brush lamb chops with oil and broil 8 minutes on each side. Season with salt and pepper. Place onion purée on a hot serving plate. Arrange lamb on the purée and serve hot.

Lamb stew

Navarin de mouton

6 servings

- 2½ pounds shoulder of lamb, cut into 3 inch cubes
- 1 tablespoon butter
- 2 tablespoons vegetable oil
- 3 onions, sliced
- 2 cloves garlic, crushed
- 2 tablespoons flour
- 1½ cups beef broth
- ½ teaspoon salt
  Freshly ground black pepper
- 1 teaspoon rosemary
- 1 bay leaf
- 12 small potatoes, peeled
- 6 carrots, sliced
- ½ turnip (optional), chopped
- 1½ pounds fresh peas in the pod or 1 package frozen peas

Brown lamb in hot butter and oil. Transfer lamb to a casserole. Sauté onions and garlic in the same skillet. Stir in flour and add beef broth. Season with salt and pepper. Add rosemary and bay leaf. Add these ingredients to the lamb. Bring broth to boiling point. Lower heat, cover and simmer for 1 hour until lamb is almost tender. Add potatoes, carrots and turnip and simmer for 20 minutes. Add peas and continue simmering another 10 minutes. Serve hot.

Cassoulet

Cassoulet

12 servings

2 pounds white Great
Northern beans
3 quarts boiling water
½ pound pork rind, if available
or ¼ pound bacon, cut
into small pieces
½ pound salt pork
2 onions, chopped
2 cloves garlic, crushed
4 sprigs parsley
2 bay leaves
1 teaspoon thyme
4 chicken bouillon cubes,
dissolved in 1 cup boiling
water
3 quarts water
1 pound Polish sausage
1 pound shoulder of lamb,
cut into 2 inch cubes
1 pound pork loin, cut into
2 inch cubes
3 tablespoons olive oil or
vegetable oil
2 onions, finely chopped
2 cloves garlic, crushed
2 stalks celery, chopped
1 cup white wine
1 cup beef broth
½ teaspoon salt
Freshly ground black pepper
4 tomatoes peeled, seeded
and chopped
1 bay leaf
1 (4½ pounds) duck
1½ cups breadcrumbs

Rinse beans and add to a large
casserole of boiling water. Boil
for 5 minutes. Remove from
the heat and allow beans to
soak for 1 hour. Cover pork
rind or bacon with 2 cups
cold water. Bring to boiling
point. Drain, rinse under cold
water and repeat this process.
Place drained beans, pork rind
or bacon, salt pork, onions,
garlic, parsley, bay leaves and
thyme and dissolved bouillon
cubes in a large casserole.
Cover with cold water. Add
Polish sausage. Simmer
uncovered for 1½ hours.
(Remove sausage after 30
minutes). Discard bay leaves.
Drain beans and reserve broth.
Brown lamb and pork in
hot oil in a large skillet. Add
onions, garlic and celery. Cook
5 minutes and add wine and
broth. Season with salt and
pepper and add tomatoes and
bay leaf. Cover and simmer
1½ hours until meat is tender.
Remove meat from the broth.
Roast the duck 1¼ hours and
cut into 2 inch pieces and
reserve 3 tablespoons fat from
duck. Place a layer of beans in
a large casserole. Add a
layer of ½ the sausage, sliced.
Add a layer of lamb, pork and
duck. Cover with more beans,
another layer of the meats,
then the remaining beans
Top with sausage. Add reserved
bean broth. There should be
enough to come almost to the
top of the beans. Add chicken
broth if there is not enough
bean liquid. Cover with a thick
layer of breadcrumbs and
drizzle with reserved duck fat.
Place over direct heat until the
broth is simmering, Place in a
350° oven for 1 hour.
This magnificently flavored
casserole involves several fairly
lengthy cooking procedures,
but none of them are difficult
and the dish can be prepared
over a period of 2 days.
However, it is best to assemble
the dish and complete the
final cooking when you are
just ready to eat it. This is an
extremely good and quite
inexpensive party dish.

*Though cassoulet began as a
humble dish, it has made its way to
the Champs Elysées. The story is
told that a shoemaker who lived in
one of the small villages of the
Languedoc called Castelnaudary,
would close his shop every
Thursday and put up a sign over
the door which read 'Closed for
reasons of cassoulet.'*

It may be more than a coincidence that the rooster is the French national symbol since in many ways the chicken is the symbol of French cooking. Napoleon's cook once wagered that he could set a different chicken dish on the table for each of the 365 days of the year. He won the bet hands down. When the 365 days were over, he had not come close to using up his inventiveness and imagination. Another convinced Frenchman saw the chicken playing a role in the art of cooking like the canvas in the art of painting. It was, he wrote, a source of inspiration from which one can create anything.

To begin with, a French chicken is never simply a chicken. Chickens are distinguished according to their place of origin. There are common chickens (which come from anywhere in France, but are always fed on corn) and superfine chickens which come from the region of Bresse in eastern France and always carry a small lead seal on the leg to designate the place of origin (just as a bottle of wine

carries a label). Secondly, a chicken is distinguished according to its age: a spring-chicken must not weigh more than three-quarters of a pound and is mostly eaten in autumn either roasted or stuffed. A roaster is a little older and must not weigh more than two pounds: it is mostly roasted or broiled and used in delicious recipes with refined sauces. Next comes the large, mature hen with white, tender flesh which is usually first braised and then stewed or poached in white wine and herbs. The hen often ends up beautifully garnished on a buffet table. Last of all comes the old rooster who has seen a lot in his well-spent life and finds a worthy end (at least from the cook's point of view) in the soup pot. Using an old rooster for this purpose is not an instance of the Frenchman's proverbial thriftiness (they are never thrifty when it comes to food), the point is that only an old rooster toughened by an adventurous life can give real body and substance to the broth.

Chicken Normandy style

Poulet Normande

4 servings

- 1 (3½ pound) chicken cut into serving pieces
- 4 tablespoons butter
- 1 tablespoon olive oil or vegetable oil
- ½ cup applejack or apple brandy, warmed
- ¼ teaspoon salt
  Freshly ground black pepper
- 4 large cooking apples, peeled, cored and thinly sliced
- 2 tablespoons flour
- ½ cup heavy cream
- ½ cup apple cider

Brown chicken in 2 tablespoons butter and oil. Flame applejack with a match and pour the flames over the chicken. Remove chicken from the heat and season with salt and pepper. Cook apples in another skillet in remaining 2 tablespoons of butter for 5 minutes until slightly softened. Place apples in a baking dish. Cover apples with chicken. Stir flour into the skillet in which chicken was cooked. Add cream and cider. Simmer 5 minutes. Spoon sauce over the chicken. Cover with aluminum foil and bake 40 minutes in a 350° oven.

Chicken in white wine

Coq au vin blanc

4 servings

- 1 (3½ pound) chicken, cut into serving pieces
- 2 tablespoons butter
- 1 tablespoon olive oil or vegetable oil
- 1 onion, finely chopped
- 1 clove garlic, crushed
- 3 tablespoons flour
- 1 cup white wine
- 1 cup chicken broth
- 1 tablespoon tomato paste
- 2 ripe tomatoes, peeled, seeded and chopped
- ½ teaspoon basil
- 1 bay leaf
- ¼ teaspoon salt
  Freshly ground black pepper
- 2 tablespoons parsley, finely chopped

Brown chicken in combined butter and oil. Transfer chicken pieces to a casserole. In the same skillet, sauté onion and garlic for 3 minutes until softened. Stir in flour and add wine and chicken broth gradually. Add tomato paste, tomatoes, basil, bay leaf, salt and pepper. Cover casserole and cook 45 minutes in a 350° oven. Garnish with parsley.

This recipe would have gladdened the heart of Henry IV, King of France from 1589-1610. His great ideal was for every Frenchman to have a chicken in the pot on Sunday, an unimaginable social and economic achievement for those times.

Chicken in wine sauce

Coq au vin

6 servings

¼ pound lean salt pork or sliced
    bacon, cut into thin strips
¼ pound carrots, sliced
18 small white onions
2 medium sized tomatoes,
    peeled, seeded and sliced
2 (2½ pound) chickens, cut
    into serving pieces
1 teaspoon salt
    Freshly ground black pepper
2 tablespoons brandy, warmed
3 tablespoons flour
3 cups red wine
½ teaspoon thyme
1 bay leaf
1 tablespoon finely chopped
    parsley
½ pound mushrooms,
    quartered if large

In a large, heavy casserole, sauté the salt pork or bacon strips until the fat is rendered. Add the carrots and onions and saute until the onions take on color, about 5 minutes. With a slotted spoon, remove the salt pork and vegetables to a side dish. Dry the pieces of chicken thoroughly with paper towels and sauté a few at a time in the hot fat until golden. Sprinkle with the salt and pepper. Ignite the brandy and pour over the chicken. When the flames die, add the tomatoes and cook 3 minutes. Return the salt pork, carrots and onions to the casserole. Sprinkle on the flour, stir, cook for a few minutes and add the wine. Bring to a boil, reduce the heat, add the thyme, bay leaf, parsley and mushrooms, cover and simmer for 30 minutes or until the chicken is tender. Serve hot from the casserole.

Braised chicken in white wine

Poulet braisé en cocotte

4 servings

- 2 (1½ pound) chickens cut into serving pieces
- 2 tablespoons butter
- 1 tablespoon olive oil or vegetable oil
- ½ pound sliced boiled ham, diced
- 1 onion, finely chopped
- 1 clove garlic, crushed
- 1 green pepper, finely chopped
- 1½ tablespoons flour
- ½ cup white wine
- ½ cup chicken broth
- 2 ripe tomatoes, peeled, seeded and chopped
- ½ teaspoon salt
  Freshly ground black pepper
- ½ teaspoon basil or marjoram
- 2 tablespoons finely chopped parsley

Brown chicken pieces in hot combined butter and oil. Transfer chicken to a casserole. Add ham to the casserole. Sauté onion, garlic and green pepper in the same butter and oil for 3 minutes. Stir in flour and add wine, chicken broth and tomatoes. Transfer all these ingredients to the casserole. Season with salt and pepper. Cover and cook 1 hour in a 300° oven. Add basil in the last ten minutes of the cooking time. Garnish with parsley and serve with rice.

Chicken with thyme

Poule au thym

4 servings

- 2 (1½ to 2 pound) fryers, halved
- 1 to 2 tablespoons dried thyme
- 1 tablespoon finely chopped parsley
- 1 teaspoon salt
  Freshly ground black pepper
- ⅓ cup oil
- ¼ cup lemon juice
- 1 clove garlic, crushed

Dry the chicken halves well with paper towels. Sprinkle them on both sides with thyme, parsley, salt and pepper. In a small bowl, combine the oil, lemon juice and garlic. Broil the chickens about 6 inches from the flame, skin side down, for 20 minutes. Brush frequently with the oil mixture. Turn the chickens and broil another 20 minutes, still brushing them with the oil. Serve hot or cold.

Chicken tarragon

Poulet à l'estragon

4 servings

- 1 (3 pound) chicken
- 1 tablespoon butter
- ½ teaspoon salt
  Freshly ground black pepper
- 1 teaspoon dried tarragon
- 2 tablespoons butter
- 2 carrots, diced
- 1 medium sized onion, finely chopped
- ½ cup chicken broth
- ½ teaspoon dried tarragon
- 1 tablespoon cornstarch, dissolved in 2 tablespoons water

Place the 1 tablespoon of butter in the cavity of the chicken. Sprinkle in the salt, pepper and tarragon and truss the chicken. Heat 2 tablespoons of butter in a heavy casserole until foaming and brown the chicken on all sides. Remove it from the pan and set aside. If the butter is too brown, discard it and melt another 2 tablespoons of butter in the casserole. Add the carrots and onion and cook until softened. Replace the chicken in the casserole on the bed of vegetables. Add the broth and ½ teaspoon of tarragon. Cover with aluminum foil, then a lid and simmer slowly on top of the stove or in a 350° oven for 50 minutes or until chicken is tender. Cut the chicken into serving pieces and place on a warmed platter. Thicken the pan juices with the cornstarch mixture. Pour the sauce with the vegetables over the chicken and serve hot.

Braised chicken in white wine

Basque chicken

Poulet à la Basquaise

4–6 servings

1 (3½ to 4 pound) chicken
3 tablespoons bacon fat or oil
1 medium onion, thinly sliced
½ teaspoon thyme
1 bay leaf
½ teaspoon salt
   Freshly ground black pepper
1 slice orange peel
2 cups chicken broth
½ pound breakfast sausage links
3 green peppers, seeded and
   cut into strips
3 medium sized tomatoes,
   peeled, seeded and sliced
½ teaspoon marjoram
½ teaspoon salt
1 tablespoon paprika
1 cup rice

In a casserole just large enough to hold the chicken, heat the bacon fat or oil and brown the chicken on all sides. Discard the fat and add the onion, thyme, bay leaf, salt, pepper, orange peel and broth. Bring to a simmer, cover and cook 45 minutes or until the chicken is tender. Meanwhile, brown the sausages in a large skillet. Drain on paper towels and slice. Pour off all but 2 tablespoons of sausage fat, or add oil if there is less than 2 tablespoons and sauté the peppers until softened. Add the tomatoes, marjoram and salt and cook about 5 minutes. Sprinkle on the paprika and cook 2 minutes more. Remove the chicken from the casserole, cut in serving pieces and wrap in foil. Keep warm in an oven heated to the lowest

Chicken in the pot

possible temperature. Strain the broth from the casserole and add water to make 2½ cups. Bring to a boil in a saucepan, add the rice, and stir once with a fork. Lower the heat, cover and simmer slowly for 25 minutes or until the broth is absorbed. Reheat

the pepper mixture and the sausage in the same pan. Place the rice on a warmed serving dish. Arrange the chicken pieces attractively on top and garnish with the peppers and sausages.

Chicken in the pot

Poule au pot

6 servings

1 (4 to 5 pound) chicken
½ pound carrots, cut into
   thick chunks
3 leeks, white part only, or
   6 scallions, sliced
2 stalks celery, roughly cut
2 turnips, roughly cut
2 large onions, quartered
4 cloves
2 teaspoons salt
   Freshly ground black pepper
½ teaspoon thyme
1 bay leaf
1 tablespoon chopped parsley
2 cloves garlic, crushed

Place all the ingredients in a large pot and cover with water. Bring to a boil and skim the broth. Lower the heat, cover and simmer 1 to 1½ hours. Carve the chicken and place it on a serving platter surrounded by the vegetables. Strain the broth and serve separately as a soup.

Chicken with olives

Poulet aux olives

4 servings

- 2 (1½ pound) chickens, cut into serving pieces
- 3 tablespoons olive oil or vegetable oil
- 2 onions, finely chopped
- 2 cloves garlic, crushed
- 2 tablespoons flour
- ½ cup white wine
- ¼ cup white vermouth
- ½ cup chicken broth
- 1 tablespoon tomato paste
- 2 tomatoes, peeled, seeded and chopped
- ½ teaspoon salt
  Freshly ground black pepper
- 1 bay leaf
- ½ teaspoon marjoram or oregano
- 8 green olives, pitted
- 8 black olives, pitted

Brown chicken in hot oil and transfer to a casserole. Sauté onions and garlic in the same oil. Stir in the flour and add the wine, vermouth and chicken broth. Add tomato paste and tomatoes. Season with salt and pepper. Add marjoram and bay leaf. Cover and cook in a 350° oven for 50 minutes. Garnish with black and green olives.

Chicken breasts with ham and cheese

Suprèmes de volaille au fromage

6 servings

- 6 whole (12 single breasts) chicken breasts
- 6 slices Proscuitto ham or thinly sliced boiled ham
- 6 thin slices Swiss or Gruyère cheese
- 1 cup flour seasoned with 1 teaspoon salt
  Freshly ground black pepper
- 3 eggs, lightly beaten
- 1 cup fine breadcrumbs
- 2 tablespoons butter
- 1 tablespoon olive oil or vegetable oil
- 3 tablespoons finely chopped parsley

Ask the butcher to remove skin and bones from each chicken breast and pound them ½ inch thick. Cut each slice of ham and cheese in half and place on each breast. Fold each breast in half. Trim ham and cheese so they fit neatly into each breast and do not protrude from the edges. Dip breasts first in seasoned flour, then into the egg and finally into the breadcrumbs. Heat butter and oil in a large skillet. Sauté breasts 6 minutes on each side until white and tender. Garnish with parsley and serve hot.

Chicken with olives

Chicken with lemon

Poulet au citron

6 servings

- 2 (2 pound) chickens, cut into serving pieces
- 2 tablespoons butter
- 1 tablespoon olive oil or vegetable oil
  Grated rind and juice of 2 lemons
- 1 teaspoon salt
  Freshly ground black pepper
- 2 tablespoons finely chopped parsley
- 2 tablespoons finely chopped chives
- 1 teaspoon marjoram
- 1 tablespoon paprika
- 2 tablespoons butter
- 1 cup chicken broth
- ¼ cup white vermouth
- 2 tablespoons cornstarch, dissolved in 3 tablespoons cold water
  Watercress or parsley for garnish

Brown chicken pieces in combined hot butter and oil. Adjust the heat to prevent the butter from burning. Transfer chicken with its cooking butter to a large baking dish. Sprinkle with lemon rind and juice. Season with salt and pepper. Cover the dish with foil and bake in a 350° oven for 45 minutes. Remove foil and add parsley, chives, marjoram and paprika. Dot chicken with butter and place under a broiler for 5 minutes until the skin is crisp and golden. Pour juices out of the dish into a saucepan. Add chicken broth and vermouth. Bring to boiling point and stir in cornstarch dissolved in cold water. Simmer 2 more minutes until sauce is thickened. Serve hot with rice. Garnish plate with watercress or parsley clusters.

Provençal chicken

Poulet Provençal

4 servings

> 1 (2½ to 3 pound) chicken
> 1 teaspoon salt
>   Freshly ground black pepper
> 1 teaspoon butter
> 2 tablespoons olive oil
> 4 cloves garlic, peeled and
>   cut in half
> ¼ teaspoon rosemary
> ½ teaspoon basil
> ¼ teaspoon thyme

Season the cavity of the chicken with ½ teaspoon of the salt, the pepper and butter. In a pan just . large enough to hold the chicken, pour in 1 tablespoon of the oil and add the garlic. Place the chicken in the pan and sprinkle it with the remaining salt, pepper, rosemary, basil, thyme and remaining olive oil. Roast the chicken in a 425° oven for 1 hour, basting frequently. Remove from the pan and cut in serving pieces. Serve hot or cold.

Cornish hens with red wine

Poulet en cocotte de grandmère

4 servings

> 4 Cornish hens
> 4 tablespoons butter
> 1 tablespoon olive oil or vegetable oil
> ½ pound bacon, fried until crisp and drained
> 2 onions, finely chopped
> 1 clove garlic, crushed
> 4 mushrooms, sliced thinly
> 2 tablespoons flour
> 1 cup beef broth
> ½ cup red wine
> 1 bay leaf
> ½ teaspoon thyme
> 3 tablespoons finely chopped parsley
> 1 teaspoon salt
> Freshly ground black pepper

Brown hens lightly in 2 tablespoons of butter and oil. Transfer hens to a large casserole. Add drained and crumbled bacon. Sauté onions and garlic in the same butter for 3 minutes. Add and sauté mushrooms until lightly browned. Stir in the flour and add beef broth and wine. Pour into the casserole and add the bay leaf, thyme and 1 tablespoon of parsley. Season with salt and pepper. Cover and cook in a 350° oven for 45 minutes. Garnish with remaining parsley. Serve with glazed onions, (see page 69) and freshly boiled new potatoes.
This dish, rich and full of flavor can also be prepared with partridge, quail, dove and other game birds in the hunting season.

Stuffed chicken or goose with apples

Poulet ou oie farcie aux pommes

6 servings

> 1 (5 pound) roasting chicken or goose
> 2 tablespoons butter, melted
> 1 pound pork sausage meat
> 2 tablespoons butter
> 2 onions, finely chopped
> 2 stalks celery, chopped
> ½ cup English walnuts, chopped
> 2 apples, peeled, cored and thinly sliced
> 1 teaspoon salt
> Freshly ground black pepper
> 1 teaspoon sage
> 1 egg, lightly beaten
> 1 (1 pound) jar small unpeeled red apples, drained
> 2 pounds fresh chestnuts (boiled) and peeled or 1 pound canned chestnuts

Cook pork sausage and drain off the accumulated fat. Heat 2 tablespoons butter in a skillet and sauté onions, celery and nuts for three minutes. Add and cook apples three minutes until slightly softened. Remove from the heat and stir in sausage meat. Season with salt, pepper and sage. Stir in the egg. Fill dressing into the chicken or goose and skewer the cavity. Brush chicken with melted butter. Place on a roasting rack and roast uncovered in a 375° oven for 2¼ hours. Simmer cooked chestnuts in boiling water for 5 minutes until they are hot. Place chicken or goose on a serving platter. Arrange apples and chestnuts around the chicken and serve hot.

Note:

Though goose is generally difficult to find in the supermarket, you may be fortunate enough to come across one at Christmas time, or ask the butcher. He might know of a source and be able to order one for you.

Stuffed chicken or goose with apples

Stuffed guinea hen

Pintadeaux farcis

4 servings

> 4 guinea hens or Cornish
> game hens with the livers
> 4 tablespoons butter
> 4 shallots or scallions, finely
> chopped
> ½ pound cottage cheese
> 4 tablespoons fine dry
> breadcrumbs
> ½ teaspoon salt
> Freshly ground black pepper
> Dash of nutmeg
> ½ teaspoon ground cloves
> ¼ teaspoon thyme
> 1 tablespoon finely chopped
> parsley
> ¾ cup dry sherry
> 2 tablespoons olive oil
> 1 cup chicken broth
> 2 bay leaves
> ¼ teaspoon salt
> 3 tablespoons heavy cream
> 2 teaspoons cornstarch,
> dissolved in 2 tablespoons
> water
> 4 slices thin white bread,
> crusts removed, and
> browned in butter

Wash the hens and dry
thoroughly. Heat 2 tablespoons
of the butter in a heavy skillet
and sauté the livers about five
minutes. Add the shallots and
cook until lightly browned.
Remove the livers, cool and chop
finely. Combine the shallots,
livers, cottage cheese, bread
crumbs, salt, pepper, nutmeg,
cloves, thyme, parsley and 1
tablespoon of the sherry and
mix thoroughly. Stuff the hens
with this mixture. Do not pack
the stuffing tightly. Close the

opening with skewers. In a heavy
casserole that is just large
enough for the 4 hens, melt
remaining butter and olive oil
until sizzling. Brown the hens
2 at a time on all sides. Pour out
the browning oil, return the
birds to the pan and add
remaining sherry, chicken broth,
bay leaves and ¼ teaspoon salt.
Bring to a simmer, drape wax
paper over the birds, cover the
pan and cook slowly about 45
minutes or until tender. Remove
the skewers and transfer the
hens to a warm serving platter,
placing each on top of a slice
of browned bread. Discard the
bay leaves from the sauce.
Boil rapidly, skimming off any
fat. Add the cream and continue
to boil until slightly syrupy.
Thicken, if desired with the
cornstarch mixture. Moisten the
hens with a little of the sauce
and pass the remainder separately.
Garnish the platter with
watercress and serve.

Duck with prunes

Canard aux pruneaux

4 servings

> 1 (4½ to 5 pound) duckling
> ½ teaspoon salt
> Freshly ground black pepper
> ½ pound dried pitted prunes
> ½ cup port wine
> 2 teaspoons lemon juice
> 4 tablespoons sugar
> 1½ cups duck stock or beef broth
> 3 tablespoons of wine vinegar
> 2 tablespoons arrowroot or
> cornstarch dissolved in 3
> tablespoons port wine

Season the cavity of the duck
with salt and pepper. Prick the
skin of the duck and place on a
rack in a roasting pan. Roast
in a 325° oven for 1½ hours.

Prick the skin occasionally and
remove excess fat from the pan.
In the meantime, combine the
prunes, ¼ cup port wine, lemon
juice and 2 tablespoons of sugar
in a bowl. Let stand until the
duck is cooked. Remove the
duck to a warmed platter. Pour
the fat out of the roasting pan,
add the bouillon and boil over
high heat scraping up the brown
pieces clinging to the pan.
Transfer the liquid to a heavy
saucepan, add the remaining
port, sugar, wine vinegar and
prune mixture. Simmer for 10
minutes. Remove the prunes with
a slotted spoon and arrange
around the duck. Thicken the
sauce with the arrowroot
mixture and spoon a little over
the duck. Serve the rest in a
separate bowl.

Duck with prunes

Duck with orange in aspic

Canards à l'orange en gelée

8 servings

 2 *(4 pound) ducks*
 5 *oranges*
 2 *teaspoons salt*
   Freshly ground black pepper
 2 *tablespoons butter, melted*
 1 *tablespoon oil*
 ½ *cup sherry or Madeira wine*
 3 *cups chicken broth*
 2 *packages (2 tablespoons)*
   unflavored gelatin dissolved
   in ⅓ cup cold water
 8 *individual prepared pastry*
   shells
 40 *thin fresh asparagus tips,*
   cooked or 2 packages frozen
   peas, cooked
 16 *black Bing cherries in*
   heavy syrup, drained

Peel 2 oranges, cut them into quarters and stuff the ducks. Season the cavity with salt and pepper. Truss ducks. Prick the skin with a fork and place on a rack in large roasting pan. Brush duck with combined oil and butter. Roast uncovered in a 350° oven for 1¼ hours. Chill the ducks. Heat wine and chicken broth in a saucepan. Pour ⅓ cup cold water into a small cup. Sprinkle gelatin powder on top of the water and allow it to stand undisturbed for 5 minutes. Add gelatin to simmering broth and stir to dissolve. Chill the broth until it is just beginning to set, about 1 hour. Pour a thin layer of wine jelly into a large serving tray. Chill and allow it to set

firmly. Place ducks on the tray and brush with half set jelly. (If the jelly becomes too firm, heat it slightly.) Allow jelly to set until firm. Peel one orange. Cut the peel into thin strips and simmer in a saucepan of boiling water for ten minutes. Drain peel and allow it to cool. Cut remaining two oranges into slices. Garnish tray with orange slices, cherries and poached orange peel. Spoon remaining jelly over the ducks and chill until serving time. Fill pastry with asparagus tips or peas and arrange on the tray.

Turkey in red wine sauce

Salpicon de dinde à la Berrichonne

6 servings

 3 *cups left over roast turkey,*
   cut into small pieces
 ½ *pound bacon, fried until*
   crisp, then crumbled
 2 *tablespoons butter*
 1 *onion, finely chopped*
 ½ *pound mushrooms, sliced*
 1 *teaspoon paprika*
 2 *tablespoons flour*
 1 *cup chicken broth*
 1 *cup red wine*
 2 *tablespoons brandy*
   (optional)
 1 *bay leaf*
 ½ *teaspoon marjoram*
   or oregano
 1 *teaspoon salt*
   Freshly ground black pepper
 2 *tablespoons finely chopped*
   parsley

Sauté onion in hot butter for three minutes until softened. Add mushrooms and cook over moderate heat for 2 minutes. Stir in the paprika and flour and add chicken broth, red wine and brandy. Place turkey and bacon in a buttered baking dish. Add bay leaf, marjoram, salt and pepper. Add the sauce. Cover and cook in a 400° oven for 15 minutes. Garnish with parsley.

Duck with orange in aspic

Turkey from Poitou

Dinde à la Poitevine

6 servings

  1 (4½ pound) turkey breast,
     boned, rolled and tied
  3 tablespoons butter
  2 medium onions, sliced
  2 cloves garlic, crushed
  2 slices bacon
  4 medium tomatoes, peeled,
     seeded and chopped
  1 teaspoon salt
     Freshly ground black pepper
  ½ teaspoon thyme
  1 tablespoon chopped parsley
  2 cups dry white wine
  2 tablespoons olive oil
  1 pound small white onions
  1 tablespoon sugar
  ¼ cup dry red wine
  ¼ cup brandy
  1 tablespoon arrowroot or
     cornstarch dissolved in
     3 tablespoons water
     Sprigs of parsley

In a large heavy casserole, melt the butter until foaming. Brown the turkey quickly on all sides. Remove to a side dish and add the onions and garlic to the pan. Cook until softened. Strain off the butter. Return the turkey to the casserole and cover with bacon to prevent it from drying out. Add the tomatoes, salt, pepper, thyme, parsley and white wine. Bring to a simmer, cover and cook slowly for 2 hours or until the meat is tender. Meanwhile, sauté the white onions in olive oil until golden. Drain off the oil and add the sugar and red wine. Cook until the liquid is syrupy. When the turkey is done, remove it from the casserole, wrap in aluminum foil and keep warm in a 200° oven. Strain the sauce and skim off the fat. Purée the onions and tomatoes in the blender or force through a sieve. Return the purée to the sauce and bring to a simmer. Add the white onions and brandy and simmer slowly 5 minutes. Thicken, with the arrowroot mixture. Slice the turkey and arrange attractively on a warmed platter. Pour the sauce over and decorate the dish with sprigs of parsley. Serve hot.

Duck with cherries

Canard Montmorency

4 servings

  1 (4 pound) duck
  ½ teaspoon salt
     Freshly ground black pepper
  2 small whole onions, peeled
  4 cloves
  1½ cups chicken broth
  ¼ teaspoon thyme
  1 bay leaf
  1 teaspoon salt
  ½ cup red port wine or other
     sweet red wine
  1 tablespoon lemon juice
  1 (1 pound) jar black pitted
     Bing cherries, drained
  2 packages (2 tablespoons)
     unflavored gelatin

Place ½ teaspoon salt, pepper and onions stuck with 4 cloves inside the duck cavity. Put the duck in a casserole. Add giblets except the liver. Add chicken broth, thyme, bay leaf and salt. Cover and simmer slowly for 1½ hours. Remove duck and discard the onions. Chill in the refrigerator. Strain the broth and chill for 4 hours. Skim off the fat from the broth. Boil broth until reduced to 1 cup. Place broth, wine, lemon juice and ½ cup drained cherry juice in a saucepan. Sprinkle the gelatin on the liquid and allow to stand undisturbed for 5 minutes. Heat over gentle heat until gelatin is dissolved. Do not allow it to boil. Chill broth in a bowl until set. Unmold jelly and chop on a board with a knife. Place the cold duck on a serving platter. Garnish with drained cherries and serve the chopped jelly separately.

Duck with cherries

Vegetable Dishes

Potatoes with cream and cheese

Gratin dauphinois

6 servings

2½ *cups heavy cream*
  2 *tablespoons butter*
  1 *clove garlic, crushed*
    Dash nutmeg
  6 *Idaho potatoes, peeled and*
    thinly sliced
½ *cup Swiss cheese, grated*
¼ *cup Parmesan cheese, grated*
½ *teaspoon salt*
    Freshly ground black pepper

Place cream, butter, garlic and
nutmeg in a small saucepan.
Simmer over low heat for 10
minutes until cream is reduced
to 2 cups and has thickened
slightly. Butter a small casserole
and arrange a layer of one third
of the potatoes in the bottom
of the dish. Add a third of the
combined cheeses, season with
salt and pepper and repeat to
form 3 layers. Dot with butter.
Add cream (There should be
enough cream to cover the
potatoes). Cover casserole and
cook in a 300° oven for 1 hour.
Serve with roast lamb.

Fried potatoes with cheese

Le truffade

2 to 3 servings

- *1 pound potatoes, peeled and thinly sliced*
- *1 tablespoon butter*
- *1 tablespoon oil*
- *2 slices bacon, diced*
- *1 clove garlic, crushed*
- *1 teaspoon salt*
  Freshly ground black pepper
  Dash of nutmeg
- *½ cup grated Cheddar cheese*

Dry the potato slices very thoroughly. In a heavy skillet, heat the butter and oil. Add the potato slices, bacon, garlic, salt, pepper and nutmeg and sauté over high heat until the potatoes are tender. Lower the heat, cover the pan and cook for 15 minutes. Uncover, raise the heat and, pressing down on the potatoes with a spatula, cook until a brown crust forms and the potatoes form a pancake. Slide the pancake onto a plate and invert back into the skillet to brown the other side. Remove from the heat and sprinkle on the cheese. Cover the skillet and allow the cheese to melt. Cut into wedges and serve hot.

Green beans

Haricots verts à la crème

6 servings

- *2 pounds green beans, cleaned and trimmed or 2 packages frozen whole green beans*
- *2 tablespoons butter*
- *1 cup heavy cream*
- *½ teaspoon salt*
  Dash of white pepper
- *1 teaspoon lemon juice*

Plunge the beans into boiling salted water and cook uncovered 8 to 10 minutes or until not quite tender. Drain and rinse under cold water so they retain their color. If using frozen beans, cook according to the package directions. Just before serving, melt the butter in a large skillet, add the beans and toss over high heat for a few minutes. Add the cream, salt and pepper and bring to a boil. Cook for about 5 minutes until the cream is reduced slightly and the beans are tender. Season with lemon juice to taste and serve hot.

Glazed onions

Oignons glaces

6 servings

- *18 small white onions, peeled*
- *2 tablespoons butter*
- *1 tablespoon olive oil or vegetable oil*
- *½ teaspoon salt*
  Freshly ground black pepper
- *1 bay leaf*
- *½ cup chicken broth*
- *2 tablespoons white vermouth*
- *2 tablespoons finely chopped parsley*

Cut a cross in the root end of each onion to prevent center from falling from the onion. Brown onions in butter and oil. Season with salt and pepper. Place onions with their cooking butter into a baking dish. Add bay leaf, chicken broth and vermouth. Cover and continue cooking in a 350° oven for 1 hour. Turn onions every 20 minutes. Garnish with parsley. Serve hot.

Glazed carrots

Carrotes Vichy

6 servings

- *12 carrots, sliced*
- *½ teaspoon salt*
- *1 tablespoon butter*
- *1 teaspoon sugar*
- *3 tablespoons white vermouth*
- *2 tablespoons finely chopped parsley*

Cover carrots with salted boiling water in a skillet. Cover and simmer 15 minutes until almost tender. Drain carrots and return them to the skillet. Add butter, sugar and vermouth. Cook uncovered for 5 minutes until the wine has evaporated and the carrots are glazed and shiny. Garnish with parsley. Serve hot.

Braised cabbage with chestnuts

Chou au marrons

6 servings

- *1 medium sized head white cabbage*
- *1 cup chicken broth*
- *1 cup dry white wine*
- *½ teaspoon salt*
- *4 thin slices cooked ham, diced*
- *10 canned chestnuts, drained and chopped*

Wash and shred the cabbage. Plunge it into boiling salted water and cook for 2 minutes. Drain and transfer to a heavy saucepan. Add broth, white wine and salt. Bring the liquid to a boil, lower the heat, cover and cook slowly 30 to 45 minutes. Before serving, stir in the ham and chestnuts.

Vegetable stew

Ratatouille

8 servings

- *1 medium sized eggplant*
- *1 tablespoon salt*
- *¼ cup olive oil or vegetable oil*
- *2 large onions, cut into rings*
- *3 cloves garlic, crushed*
- *2 green peppers, cut into strips*
- *4 medium sized zucchini, cut into bite-sized pieces*
- *2 medium sized ripe tomatoes, cut into wedges*
- *¼ teaspoon salt*
  Freshly ground black pepper
- *½ teaspoon thyme*
- *1 bay leaf*
- *2 tablespoons parsley, finely chopped*

Cut eggplant into thick slices and then into small pieces. Sprinkle with salt. Allow eggplant to stand for 30 minutes, then rinse and pat dry on paper towels. Heat the oil in a large skillet. Sauté onions and garlic for two minutes. Add green pepper and cook for two minutes. Add eggplant and cook over high heat for three minutes, stirring constantly. Add zucchini and continue stirring for three minutes. Add tomatoes, salt, pepper, thyme and bay leaf. Simmer uncovered for 40 minutes until all the vegetables are tender. Remove bay leaf. Garnish with parsley and serve hot.
Ratatouille can also be served cold as an appetizer.

Endives au gratin

Endives au lard gratinées

4 servings

- *8 endives*
- *4 slices bacon*
- *1 tablespoon butter*
- *2 cups Bechamel sauce (see page 35)*
- *½ cup Parmesan cheese, grated*

Cut a V shaped notch in the base of each endive and wash carefully. Simmer whole endives in salted water for 20 minutes. Fry bacon until almost crisp and all the fat has rendered. Cut each bacon slice in half across the width. Wrap each endive in bacon. Place in a buttered baking dish.* Spoon sauce over the endives. Top with cheese and bake in a 375° oven for 15 minutes until lightly browned. Serve hot with roast lamb or chicken.
*Can be prepared in advance to this point.

Vegetable stew

Asparagus with ham

Asperges au jambon

6 servings

- 2 pounds fresh asparagus
- ½ teaspoon salt
- 2 tablespoons lemon juice
- 6 thin slices boiled ham
  Hollandaise sauce (page 34)

Peel lower third of asparagus spears with a potato peeler. Place asparagus in a large skillet. Cover with cold water. Add salt and lemon juice. Simmer uncovered 10 minutes until tender. Place a piece of ham on each individual serving dish. Cover with drained asparagus and spoon Hollandaise sauce over asparagus. Serve immediately.

Pumpkin au gratin

Potiron au gratin

4 to 6 servings

- 1 can (1 pound) pumpkin
- ½ teaspoon salt
  Freshly ground black pepper
  Dash of nutmeg
- ¼ teaspoon ground cloves
- 2 tablespoons melted butter
- 1 egg
- ½ cup heavy cream
- 2 tablespoons grated Parmesan cheese

Thoroughly combine the pumpkin, salt, pepper, nutmeg, cloves and butter. Place in a small, lightly buttered casserole. Beat the egg lightly and mix in the cream and Parmesan cheese. Pour over the pumpkin. Bake in a 400° oven 30 minutes or until the top is puffed and lightly browned. Serve warm.

The large orange pumpkin ripens at the same time as the grapes and always grows along the edges of the vineyard. Soup made from this pumpkin is a traditional dish served to grape-pickers.

Stuffed tomatoes Riviera style

Tomates farcies à la Nicoise

4 servings

- 4 medium sized tomatoes
- ¼ pound ground beef, cooked and cooled
- 1 medium sized onion, finely chopped
- 1 clove garlic, crushed
- 1 medium sized potato, cooked and mashed
- 1 tablespoon finely chopped parsley
- ¼ teaspoon salt
  Freshly ground black pepper
- 1 egg, lightly beaten
- 1 tablespoon olive oil or salad oil
- ¼ cup fine breadcrumbs
- 2 tablespoons butter

Slice the top off each tomato and scoop out the pulp with a teaspoon. Place tomato pulp, beef, onion, garlic, potato, parsley, salt and pepper in a bowl. Combine with the egg and olive oil. Fill mixture into tomatoes. Sprinkle each with breadcrumbs and top with a pat of butter. Bake in a buttered baking dish in a 350° oven for 20 minutes. Serve hot.

Stuffed mushrooms

Champignons à la Bordelaise

4 servings

- 1 pound fresh mushrooms
- 2 tablespoons butter
- 2 tablespoons olive oil or vegetable oil
- 4 scallions, finely chopped
- 2 cloves garlic, crushed
- 3 tablespoons parsley, finely chopped
- ¼ teaspoon salt
  Freshly ground black pepper
- 2 tablespoons lemon juice
- ¼ cup heavy cream
- ¼ cup fine breadcrumbs

Wash mushrooms quickly under cold running water and pat them dry on paper towels. Remove the stems from the caps. Sauté mushroom caps in hot butter for two minutes on each side until lightly browned. Place caps in a buttered baking dish, hollow side up. Add oil to the skillet. Chop mushroom stems finely. Combine with scallions, garlic and parsley. Season with salt and pepper. Sauté mushroom mixture in hot oil and butter for five minutes.
Add lemon juice and cream. Simmer five more minutes. Fill this mixture into mushroom caps and top with breadcrumbs. Bake 5 minutes in a 400° oven just before serving. Serve hot on freshly made toast.

Sautéed mushrooms country style

Cèpes sautés paysanne

4–6 servings

>   6 slices bacon
>   2 pounds cépes or mushrooms
>   1 teaspoon lemon juice
>   1 small onion, finely chopped
>   1 clove garlic, crushed
>   2 tablespoons fine dry
>   breadcrumbs
>   ½ teaspoon salt
>   Freshly ground black pepper
>   1 tablespoon finely chopped
>   parsley

In a large skillet, cook the bacon over low heat until crisp. Drain and crumble. In the pan in which the bacon was cooked, sauté the mushrooms for 3 minutes in the remaining fat. Adding a little butter if necessary. Sprinkle with lemon juice. Add the onion, garlic and breadcrumbs, and sauté over high heat, stirring constantly, for 3 minutes. Add the bacon, salt, pepper and parsley and mix well. Serve hot.

Note: Cépes are one of the many types of mushrooms found in France, Italy and Germany. They are available here both dried and in cans. If you are unable to find any, use fresh mushrooms for this dish. Serve with roast beef.

Large brown cèpes (a kind of mushroom) grow in the extensive pinewood forest located near the city of Bordeaux. On Sundays whole families leave Bordeaux with baskets and pick their way among the trees to look for them.

Chocolate mousse

Mousse au chocolat

6 servings

- ¼ *pound bitter or semisweet chocolate*
- *4 egg yolks*
- *4 egg whites*
- *4 tablespoons butter, softened*
- *2 tablespoons Grand Marnier*

Break chocolate into small pieces and put on a plate. Cover with another plate. Put the plates over a saucepan of simmering water and leave for 10 minutes until the chocolate has melted. Beat the egg yolks in a mixer until they are very thick. Fold in the butter, orange liquer and melted chocolate. Beat the egg whites until they stand in soft peaks. Fold chocolate mixture into the egg whites with a wooden spoon. Divide mixture between six small dishes. Chill four hours before serving.

Chocolate mousse

Bavarian coffee-cream

Moka parfait

4 servings

- 1¼ *cups milk*
- ½ *cup whole dark roast coffee beans or 1½ teaspoons instant coffee*
- *3 egg yolks*
- ⅓ *cup sugar*
- ⅓ *cup water*
- *1 package unflavored gelatin*
- *1 teaspoon sugar*
- *1 tablespoon Kahlua or other coffee liquer*
- *1 cup heavy cream, partially whipped*
  Grated sweet chocolate

Scald the milk with the coffee beans. Beat the egg yolks with the sugar until very thick and mousse-like. Strain the milk and beat into the egg yolks. Return the mixture to the pan and cook, stirring constantly, over low heat until the mixture thickens. Allow the mixture to cool for 10 minutes. Sprinkle the gelatin over the water to soften. Add 1 teaspoon sugar and place over gentle heat, stirring to melt the gelatin. Add the gelatin and Kahlua to the cooled egg mixture. Fold in the cream. Pour into small individual molds and refrigerate at least 3 hours. Decorate with grated sweet chocolate before serving.

Pear sundaes

Pear sundaes

Poires Belle-Hélène

6 servings

  6 *Anjou pears, peeled and cored*
  1 *cup sugar*
2½ *cups water*
  1 *tablespoon lemon juice*
  1 *vanilla bean or 1 teaspoon*
     vanilla extract
  1 *pint vanilla ice cream*
  ½ *cup sliced almonds*

Sauce:
  ½ *pound sweet or semi-sweet*
     chocolate
  ½ *cup water*
  1 *tablespoon cornstarch,*
     dissolved in 2 tablespoons
     cold water
  1 *tablespoon butter, softened*

Place sugar, water, lemon juice and vanilla bean in a heavy saucepan. Bring to boiling point and simmer for 5 minutes. Lower the pears into the syrup and poach pears uncovered for 15 minutes. Remove from the heat and allow pears to cool in the syrup. Add vanilla extract if bean was not used. To prepare the sauce: Melt chocolate in the water, stirring until smooth. Stir in cornstarch dissolved in cold water and add the butter. To complete the dish: Put the ice cream in a chilled bowl or individual serving dishes. Stand a pear on the ice cream and pour warm chocolate sauce over the pear. Sprinkle with sliced almonds and serve at once.

Grand Marnier soufflé

Soufflé au Grand Marnier

4 servings

2½ *tablespoons butter*
  3 *tablespoons flour*
  1 *cup milk*
  ¼ *cup sugar*
  4 *egg yolks*
  ¼ *cup Grand Marnier*
  1 *teaspoon vanilla*
  6 *egg whites*
     Pinch of salt
  ⅛ *teaspoon cream of tartar*
  3 *tablespoons confectioners*
     sugar, sifted

In a heavy saucepan, melt the butter and add the flour. Cook, stirring for 1 to 2 minutes. Add the milk gradually, beating with a wire whisk. Add the sugar and cook several minutes to form a thick sauce. Remove the pan from the heat and beat in the egg yolks one at a time. Add the Grand Marnier and vanilla. Beat the egg whites with the salt and cream of tartar until stiff peaks form. Stir ¼ of the egg whites into the yolk mixture and carefully fold in the remainder. Butter and sugar a 1½ to 2 quart soufflé dish or other straight sided mold. Place the egg mixture in the dish and bake in a 400° oven for 10 minutes. Lower the heat to 350° and bake 20 minutes more or until the soufflé is puffed and golden. Sprinkle with confectioners sugar and serve immediately.

In France, very thin, light pancakes are called 'crêpes'. These pancakes originally come from Brittany, where they are still a kind of national dish. In all the small villages and towns of this picturesque province one can find 'crêperies', small restaurants which specialize in these delicious pancakes.

Old Breton women, sometimes still wearing the traditional square white caps, stand behind the stove and manipulate these delicate treats. Crêpes are eaten with all kinds of fillings, both hearty and sweet: with ham, meat or shrimp, and with honey and fruit. In the crêperies of Brittany crêpes are almost always accompanied by cider, the light, sparkling apple wine of the region. The most famous crêpes in France are the 'crêpes Suzette', known all over the world as a very special dessert. According to tradition crêpes Suzette were created some time during the last century by the owner of a small restaurant in Paris located near the Comédie Francaise theater. He is supposed to have gotten the inspiration from a very successful play in which the maid, called Suzette, appeared carrying a tray of crêpes. To amuse his theatergoing customers, the owner of the restaurant prepared pancakes drenched in orange liqueur, which he called crêpes Suzette. The recipe caught on and the crêpes Suzette, in all its variations, has become one of the world's best known desserts.

Crêpes with honey

Crêpes au miel

6 servings

1¼ cups milk
1 egg
1 egg yolk
1 tablespoon butter, melted
¼ teaspoon salt
2 tablespoons sugar
1 cup sifted all purpose flour
  or wheat flour
1 tablespoon vegetable oil
½ cup honey
6 tablespoons butter

Place milk, egg, egg yolk, 4 tablespoons of butter, salt, sugar and flour in a blender. Blend one minute until the batter is smooth. Heat oil in a small (5½ inch base) frying pan or crêpe pan. Pour in a spoonful of batter. Rotate the pan in all directions to cover the cooking surface evenly. Tip out any excess batter. Cook one minute until crêpe is lightly browned. Turn and brown on the second side. (Discard the first crêpe which will be oily). Place a teaspoon of butter and honey on each crêpe. Fold and serve hot.

Crêpes suzettes

Crêpes Suzettes

9 servings
18 crêpes

Batter:
1¼ cups milk
1 egg
1 egg yolk
1 tablespoon butter, melted
¼ teaspoon salt
2 tablespoons sugar
1 cup sifted all purpose flour
1 tablespoon vegetable oil

Sauce:
3 tablespoons butter
3 tablespoons sugar
  Rind of one orange
  Juice of two oranges
2 tablespoons Grand Marnier or
  other orange liquer

Place milk, egg, egg yolk, butter, salt, sugar and flour in a blender. Blend one minute until smooth. Oil frying pan and prepare crêpes following the directions **for crêpes with honey, this page** Heat butter in a large skillet. Stir in sugar, orange rind and juice. Roll prepared crêpes in the sauce. Fold each crêpe into half and then half again. Arrange crêpes over the surface of the skillet. Add Grand Marnier. Light with a match and serve flaming.

Crêpes with apples

Crêpes aux pommes

6 servings
12 crêpes

Batter:
1¼ cups milk
1 egg
1 egg yolk
1 tablespoon butter, melted
¼ teaspoon salt
2 tablespoons sugar
1 cup sifted all purpose flour

Filling:
2 tablespoons butter
3 medium sized cooking apples,
  peeled and cored
2 tablespoons sugar
  Rind and juice of 1 lemon
⅛ teaspoon cinnamon
  Dash nutmeg
1 tablespoon butter
3 tablespoons confectioners
  sugar
1 cup heavy cream
2 tablespoons sugar
1 teaspoon vanilla

Place all the batter ingredients in a blender in the order listed. Blend one minute until smooth. Prepare crêpes following the directions for **crêpes with honey, this page. Slice apples thinly;** cut into small pieces. Fry apples in 2 tablespoons butter until slightly softened, adding sugar, lemon rind and juice, cinnamon and nutmeg. Fill apples into crêpes and roll crêpes like a cigarette. Butter a baking dish. Place the crêpes in the dish and dot with remaining butter. Place in a 350° oven for 10 minutes. Dust crêpes with sifted confectioners sugar just before serving. Serve with heavy cream combined with sugar and vanilla.

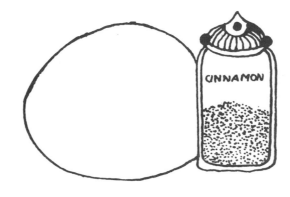

Baked cherries

Clafouti aux Cerises

6 servings

3 cups	**sweet cherries**
1¼ cups	milk
4	eggs
½ cup	sugar
1 teaspoon	salt
1 cup	flour
1½ tablespoons	butter, melted
¼ cup	confectioners sugar

Remove pits from the **cherries,** and place in an 8 cup baking dish. Combine remaining ingredients, except the confectioners sugar, in a blender. Blend until smooth. Pour batter **over the cherries and bake 30** minutes in a 350° oven. Dust surface with sifted confectioners sugar and serve hot.

This dessert can be made with plums, peaches, apples or other fruits in season. It is particularly good served with whipped cream.

Cherries in brandy

Cerises à l'eau de vie

4 *pounds slightly unripe cherries*
4 *cups (1 quart) brandy*
2 *cups sugar*
¼ *cup water*

Remove the stems from the cherries. Put the cherries in glass jars. Pour in the brandy. Put the lids on the jars and leave for 6 weeks in a warm, preferably sunny, place. Pour the brandy from the cherries into a jug. Combine sugar and water and boil uncovered for 5 minutes. Cool the syrup and add to the brandy. Pour back over the cherries. Close the jars again and place in a warm place for 14 days before serving. Serve with ice cream.

Peaches in white wine

Pêches au vin

4 servings

4 *large ripe peaches*
4 *teaspoons quick dissolving sugar*
8 *tablespoons sweet white wine*

Drop the peaches into boiling water for 15 seconds. Drain and rinse them under cold water. Remove the skins and slice each into a large wine glass. Sprinkle each serving, with 1 teaspoon sugar and add 2 tablespoons wine. Let stand at least ½ hour before serving.

Strawberries Romanoff

Fraises Romanoff

4 servings

1 *(1 quart) box strawberries*
3 *tablespoons sugar*
2 *large naval oranges*
2 *tablespoons Grand Marnier*
1 *tablespoon brandy*
   whipped cream

Remove the stems from the strawberries and rinse quickly under cold water. Dry the strawberries on paper towels. Place in a serving dish and sprinkle with sugar. Peel the oranges. Cut into segments cutting between the membranes. Add orange segments to strawberries. Squeeze orange juice from remaining pulp over the strawberries. Add Grand **Marnier and brandy. Serve with whipped cream.**

Pineapple flambéed in Kirsch

Ananas flambé

4 servings

1 *small fresh pineapple or 1 (1 pound 14 ounce) can pineapple rings, drained*
3 *tablespoons butter*
4 *tablespoons sugar*
¼ *cup Kirsch, warmed*
4 *scoops vanilla ice cream*

Trim pineapple and cut into 8 rings. Melt the butter in a large skillet. Add pineapple. Sprinkle with half of the sugar and cook over high heat until lightly browned. Turn pineapple on to the second side, sprinkle with remaining sugar and continue cooking until lightly browned. Add Kirsch and light with a match. When the flames have died down, serve hot pineapple on a scoop of ice cream in individual serving dishes. Pour pan juices over the pineapple.

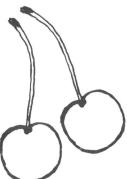

Cold lemon soufflé

Soufflé au citron

8 servings

- 5 eggs
- 1½ cups sugar
  Juice (¾ cup) and grated rind of 3 large lemons
- 2 packages gelatin
- ½ cup water
- 1 teaspoon sugar
- 2 cups heavy cream, partially whipped
  Pinch of salt
- ⅛ teaspoon cream of tartar
- ¼ cup macaroon crumbs or toasted ground almonds
- ¾ cup heavy cream, whipped
- 2 tablespoons ground pistachio nuts

Butter and sugar a 1½ quart soufflé dish or other straight sided mold. Tie a collar of oiled and sugared wax paper or aluminum foil around the mold to extend the sides. (Be sure to oil the collar. Butter will solidify when chilled and the soufflé will stick to the paper.) Separate the eggs and beat the yolks with the sugar and lemon rind, adding the lemon juice gradually, until the mixture is very thick and mousse-like. Do not underbeat. Sprinkle the gelatin over the water to soften. Add 1 teaspoon sugar and stir over low heat to dissolve the gelatin. Cool and add to the lemon mixture, combining thoroughly. Fold in the partially whipped cream. Beat the egg whites with the salt and cream of tartar until stiff peaks form. Fold into the lemon mixture. Turn into the prepared soufflé dish and chill in the refrigerator until set. Remove the collar and decorate the sides of the soufflé with macaroon crumbs and the top with the whipped cream and pistachio nuts.

Apple omelette

Omelette Normande

4 servings

- 3 small tart apples, peeled, cored and sliced thinly
  Juice of one lemon
- 4 tablespoons butter
- 2 tablespoons superfine sugar
- ¼ teaspoon cinnamon
  Dash of nutmeg
- 1 tablespoon apple brandy
- 6 eggs
- 3 tablespoons apple brandy, warmed
- ½ cup heavy cream, whipped and sweetened with 1 tablespoon sugar

Sprinkle the apple slices with lemon juice. Melt 2 tablespoons of the butter in a skillet and sauté the apples until soft. Add 1 tablespoon of the sugar, the cinnamon, nutmeg and 1 tablespoon apple brandy. Keep the mixture warm. Stir the eggs together lightly with a fork. In a 10 inch omelette pan or skillet with rounded sides, melt the remaining butter. When very hot, pour in the eggs and stir vigorously with a fork until partially set. Place the apple mixture on one half of the omelette and fold over the other half. Let the omelette brown for a few seconds and turn out onto a serving dish. Sprinkle with the remaining sugar. Heat a metal skewer until very hot and burn a cross design on the omelette. Ignite the warmed apple brandy, and pour the flames over the omelette. Serve with sweetened whipped cream.

Caramel custard

Crème caramel

6 servings

For the caramel:
- 2 tablespoons water
- ½ cup sugar

For the custard:
- 2 cups milk, scalded
- 1 teaspoon vanilla
- 4 eggs
- ¾ cup sugar

Have 6 small (½ cup) ovenproof molds ready. In a small heavy saucepan, preferably enameled, place the sugar and water. Bring to a boil, swirling the mixture until the sugar dissolves. Cook until the mixture is a deep, golden brown. (Watch carefully so the caramel is not allowed to burn.) Immediately remove the pan from the heat and hold it in a basin of water for 10 seconds to stop the cooking. Pour a layer of caramel into each mold. Add vanilla to the scalded milk. Beat the eggs together with the sugar until well combined. Stirring constantly, strain the warm milk into the eggs. Pour the custard into the molds. Place the molds in a shallow pan and add water to come halfway up the sides of the molds. Place in a 350° oven and bake for 35 minutes or until custard is set. Chill for 2 hours. Run a knife around the inside of each mold and invert the custard on individual dessert plates.

Peach Melba

Pêche Melba

4 servings

- 2 large ripe peaches
- 1 cup sugar
- 2 cups water
- ½ vanilla bean or 1 teaspoon vanilla extract
- 1 package frozen raspberries
- 4 scoops vanilla ice cream
- 4 tablespoons, sliced almonds, toasted 5 minutes on a cookie sheet in a 350° oven

Dissolve sugar in water in a small saucepan over low heat. Split vanilla bean in half lengthwise. Scrape inner part into the syrup and add the remaining part. Simmer five minutes. Add whole peaches and simmer five minutes. Drain peaches and remove the skin. Cut each peach in half. Add vanilla extract to syrup if vanilla bean was not used. Allow peaches to cool in the syrup. Thaw raspberries. Drain raspberries and reserve syrup. Force through a strainer. Add ⅓ cup of raspberry syrup to form a thick sauce. Place a scoop of ice cream in 4 serving dishes. Add drained poached peach half. Top with raspberry sauce and scatter each dish with cooled, toasted almonds.

This dessert, sublimely simple, was created in 1893 by the famous French chef, Escoffier, who was then head cook at the elegant Savoy in London. He named it in honor of the world-famous Australian opera singer, Nellie Melba.

Empress rice

Riz à l'impératrice

8 servings

- ¾ cup diced candied fruits
- 4 tablespoons Kirsch
- 2 cups milk
- 1 vanilla bean, split or 1 teaspoon vanilla extract
- ½ cup uncooked rice
- ½ cup sugar
- ½ cup dried apricots, cooked for 30 minutes then drained
- 1 package unflavored gelatin
- ¼ cup water
- 1 teaspoon sugar
- ½ cup red currant jelly
- 1¼ cups heavy cream, partially whipped

Combine the candied fruits and Kirsch in a small bowl and let stand while preparing the rice. In a large saucepan, bring the milk to a simmer with the vanilla bean. Add the rice, stir and simmer slowly until the rice is tender. Remove from the heat, discard the vanilla bean or add vanilla extract if bean was not used. Stir in the sugar. Add the marinated fruits. Purée the apricots in a blender and force through a sieve to remove the skins. Add to the rice. Sprinkle the gelatin over the water to soften. Add the 1 teaspoon sugar and place over gentle heat, stirring to melt the gelatin. Add it to the rice and mix well. Set in the refrigerator to cool, stirring every 15 minutes to suspend the fruits in the mixture. Oil a 1½ quart mold and place a circle of wax paper on the bottom. Melt the red currant jelly and pour into the mold. Place in the freezer a few minutes to set the jelly. When the rice mixture has started to set slightly, fold in the cream and turn the mixture into the mold. Cover with a circle of oiled wax paper and refrigerate overnight. Run a knife around the edge of the mold and invert the rice on a serving plate.

Plum compôte

Compôte de pruneaux

4 servings

- 2 pounds plums with pits removed
- ½ cup sugar
- ¼ cup water
  Rind and juice of 1 orange
- ½ cup Port wine or other sweet red wine
- 2 tablespoons red currant jelly
- ½ teaspoon almond extract
- ½ cup sliced almonds

Place all the ingredients except the almond extract and almonds in a saucepan. Cover and simmer over low heat for 20 minutes. Add almond extract. Chill for 4 hours. Sprinkle with sliced almonds just before serving.

Sweet bread

Fouasse

1 package dry yeast
¼ cup lukewarm water
1 cup milk
1 egg
½ cup sugar
½ teaspoon cinnamon
1 teaspoon salt
6 tablespoons melted butter
4 to 4½ cups all purpose flour

In a small bowl, sprinkle the yeast over the water. Stir to dissolve. Heat the milk to lukewarm. In a large bowl, combine the egg, sugar, cinnamon and salt, beating until well combined. Add the yeast, milk and 4 tablespoons of the butter and beat again. Stir in the flour gradually until the dough can be gathered into a soft ball. Blend in the remaining flour with your fingers. Turn the dough out onto a lightly floured board and knead until smooth and elastic. The dough will be soft. To prevent sticking, rub your hands occasionally with some of the remaining butter but do not add more flour. Place the dough in a lightly oiled bowl, cover and let rise in a warm place until doubled. Punch the dough down and knead a few times. Divide it into 3 pieces and roll each piece between your hands into a long rope. Braid the ropes, pinching the ends together. Form the braid into a ring and place on an oiled baking sheet. Cover and let rise again until double. Bake in a 350° oven for 35 to 40 minutes.

Corn cake

Millar

6 servings

1 teaspoon butter
1 tablespoon flour
1¼ cups sugar
5 egg yolks
¾ cup sifted all purpose flour
2 cups milk, simmering
1 (12 ounce) can golden corn
Rind from 1 orange, finely grated
Rind from 1 lemon, finely grated
1 teaspoon vanilla
5 egg whites

Butter and flour a 1½ quart soufflé dish or 9 inch cake tin. Beat 1¼ cups sugar and the egg yolks until very thick. Beat in the flour. Stir in simmering milk. Place in saucepan and heat until thickened into a custard. Add corn and grated orange rind, lemon rind and vanilla. Beat egg whites until they stand in soft peaks. Fold custard into egg whites. Place in the prepared dish and bake in a 375° oven for 25 minutes. Serve immediately.

Flambéed cherries

Cerises flambées

6 servings

1 pound fresh cherries or
1 (1 pound) jar Bing cherries, pitted
½ cup water
1 cup sugar
1 tablespoon arrowroot or cornstarch, dissolved in 2 tablespoons cold water
1 teaspoon vanilla extract
1 tablespoon cherry brandy
¼ cup brandy, warmed

Remove stems and pits from fresh cherries. Simmer water and sugar in a saucepan for five minutes. Add cherries and simmer five more minutes. (Or simmer canned cherries in ¾ cup of cherry juice.) Remove cherries with a slotted spoon. Add cornstarch paste to syrup and cook one minute until thickened. Remove pan from the heat. Add vanilla and cherry brandy. Pour warmed brandy over cherries. Light with a match and serve flaming cherries with ice cream.
Other fruit can also be flamed in this manner: e.g. apricots flavored with apricot brandy and flamed with kirsch; peaches flavored with peach brandy and flamed with white rum, pears flavored with crème de cacao and flamed with dark rum.

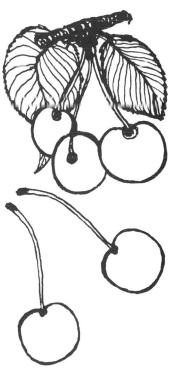

Chestnut block

Pavé aux marrons

6 servings

- ¾ cup sugar
- 3 tablespoons water
- ¼ cup softened butter
- 1 cup canned unsweetened chestnut purée

For the frosting:
- 2 squares unsweetened chocolate
- 1½ tablespoons sugar
- 3 tablespoons water
- ¼ cup butter

In a small pan, boil the sugar and water together to make a syrup. Beat the softened butter into the chestnut purée. Stir in the syrup. Oil a small loaf pan and line with a strip of wax paper long enough to hang over the long sides of the pan by 2 inches. Pour the chestnut mixture into the pan and freeze until set. To prepare the frosting, combine the chocolate, sugar, water and butter in a small saucepan. Stir over low heat until the chocolate is melted. Cool the frosting until it is of spreading consistency. Remove the chestnut mixture from the refrigerator. Run a knife along the sides of the pan and invert onto a serving plate. Spread the frosting evenly over the top and sides of the block with a spatula. Let the frosting solidify a few minutes. Slice and serve.

Grape cake

Grape cake

Gâteau aux raisins

8 servings

- 2 cups water
- 8 tablespoons butter cut into small pieces
- ½ teaspoon salt
- 2 tablespoons sugar
- 2 cups all purpose flour
- 8 eggs

Filling:
- 1 cup sugar
- 5 egg yolks
- ¾ cup flour
- 1 cup milk, simmering
- 1 cup heavy cream, simmering
- 1 teaspoon vanilla extract
- 1 small bunch white grapes
- 1 small bunch black grapes

Place water, butter, salt and sugar in a heavy saucepan. Adjust the heat so that the butter has completely melted when the water boils. Remove the pan from the heat as soon as the water boils. Add the flour all at once and stir vigorously. Return the pan to a moderate heat for two minutes until the dough can be formed into a ball. Remove the pan from the heat and add the eggs one at a time. Beat each egg well into the mixture before adding the next egg. Butter and flour three cookie sheets and draw three 9 inch circles in the flour using a plate as a guide. Spread the mixture within the circles as smoothly as possible. Bake 20 minutes in a 350 degree oven. Turn the oven off and leave the layers in the oven for another five minutes. Remove and allow the layers to cool. In the meantime, prepare the custard. Beat the sugar and eggs together until thick and lemon colored. Beat in the flour. Stir in the combined simmering milk and cream. Place in a saucepan over moderate heat and stir continuously with a wire whisk to form a thick custard. Add the vanilla and cool the custard. To assemble the cake, place one third of the firm, cool custard on the bottom layer and cover with a layer of white and black grapes. Continue with the second layer and arrange the grapes attractively on the top layer. Allow the cake to stand for 1 hour before cutting.

Normandy style apple pie

Tarte aux pommes Normande

6 servings

- 9 inch unbaked pastry shell (use 1 package frozen patty shells, thawed and rolled into a circle, or pastry recipe on page 89) or 1 prepared unbaked pie shell
- 4 cups prepared applesauce
- ⅓ cup sugar
- 2 tablespoons apple jack, apple brandy or brandy, (optional)
- 1 package unflavored gelatin
- 3 cooking apples, peeled, cored and sliced thinly
- 3 tablespoons sugar
- 1 tablespoon lemon juice
- 1 tablespoon butter
- ½ cup apricot preserves, heated and strained
- 1 cup heavy cream
- 2 tablespoons sugar
- 1 teaspoon vanilla extract

Fit pastry into a 9 inch pie plate. Prick with a fork and bake in a 400° oven for 15 minutes. Place applesauce, sugar and brandy in a small skillet. Cook over moderate heat for 15 minutes until thick. Stir to prevent applesauce from sticking to the pan. Place ⅓ cup cold water in a saucepan. Sprinkle gelatin on the water. Allow it to stand undisturbed for 5 minutes. Place pan over low heat until gelatin has dissolved. Stir gelatin into applesauce and then fill pastry shell. Cover applesauce with apple slices. Sprinkle with sugar and lemon juice and dot with butter. Bake in a 375° oven for 30 minutes. Brush apples with clear warm liquid from strained apricot preserves. Chill for 4 hours before serving. Whip the cream until it is slightly thickened. Add the sugar and vanilla. Continue beating until very thick. Serve apple pie and whipped cream separately.

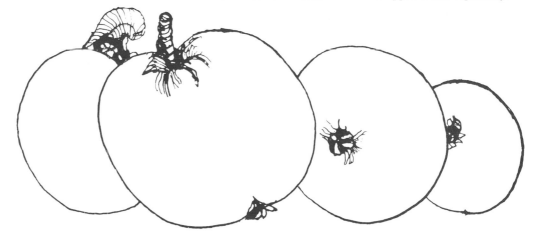

Strawberry meringue

Strawberry meringue

Vacherin aux fraises

10 servings

6 egg whites
⅛ teaspoon cream of tartar
1 teaspoon salt
1 teaspoon vanilla
1½ cups granulated sugar
1 quart vanilla ice cream
½ pound strawberries
½ cup red currant jelly, melted

Butter and flour 4 cookie sheets or cover each with a sheet of parchment paper. Outline 4–7 inch circles using a plate as a guide. Place egg whites, cream of tartar, salt and vanilla in a large mixing bowl. Beat until egg whites stand in soft peaks. Add sugar a spoonful at a time. Continue beating until egg whites are stiff. Spoon egg whites into a large pastry bag fitted with a No. 5 star tube. Outline 3 circles with egg whites. Outline fourth circle in the same way but fill in the circle completely with inward radiating rings of egg white. Reserve remaining egg whites. Bake meringues in a 200° oven for 1 hour. Without opening the oven door, turn oven off and leave meringues to dry for 1 hour more. Remove meringues from the oven. On a clean, buttered and floured cookie sheet, place rings on top of each other using remaining meringue to hold circles in place. Decorate outside of meringue case with rosettes of meringue. Return meringue case to a 200° oven and bake for 1 hour. Turn oven off and leave meringue for 1 hour more until it has dried completely. Fill meringue case with ice cream and a few sliced strawberries. Arrange remaining strawberries on top of the ice cream and brush with melted red currant jelly.
The meringue shell can be prepared 3 or 4 days in advance and the dessert assembled just before serving.

Christmas log

Bûche de Noël

10 servings

Batter:
8 eggs
1 cup sugar
1 cup ground blanched almonds
1 cup all purpose flour

Syrup:
1 cup water
1 cup sugar
2 tablespoons Kirsch

Cream:
4 egg yolks
1 cup sugar
¼ cup water
1 cup butter, creamed
3 ounces unsweetened redi-blend chocolate

Decoration:
Powdered sugar

Beat the eggs and sugar together until very thick and mousse like. The mixture will at least triple in volume. Carefully fold in the almonds and flour. Oil a jelly roll pan, 15½ × 10½ × 1. Line it with a sheet of wax paper longer than the pan. Oil the paper. Turn the batter into the pan and spread it evenly. Bake in a 350° oven 20 to 25 minutes or until it tests done. Meanwhile, combine the sugar and water for the syrup and boil until the sugar is dissolved.

Cool completely and add the Kirsch. Place 2 overlapping sheets of wax paper on a board and dust them with powdered sugar. Invert the cake on the paper and peel off the wax paper on which the cake was baked. When the cake is cool, brush on the syrup. Add a little at a time until all the syrup is used. Beat the egg yolks in a bowl until thick and creamy. Boil the sugar and ¼ cup water together until the mixture reaches 235° on a candy thermometer or a soft ball forms when a few drops are put into cold water. Beating constantly, pour the hot syrup into the egg yolks in a thin, steady stream. Continue beating a few minutes. Beat in the creamed butter. Reserve 2 tablespoons of the butter cream and beat the chocolate into the remainder. Spread the cake with a thin layer of chocolate buttercream. Beginning at one long edge, roll the cake up onto a long board or serving plate using the wax paper as an aid. Round off the ends and spread them with the white buttercream. Spread the top and sides of the log with the remaining chocolate buttercream. Run the tines of a fork over the buttercream to resemble bark. Sift on a little powdered sugar. Decorate the log with marzipan holly leaves and candied cherries.

Mocha cake

Moka gâteau

8 servings

 1 cup sifted all purpose flour
 ¼ teaspoon salt
 4 eggs
 ¾ cup sugar
 1 teaspoon instant coffee
 ⅔ cup ground almonds
   with skins
 ½ cup apricot preserves
 1 cup heavy cream
 2 tablespoons sugar
 1 teaspoon instant coffee
 1 can (1 pound 14 ounces)
   apricot halves, drained
 ½ cup ground toasted almonds

Butter and flour a 9 inch cake pan. Line the bottom with a circle of buttered wax paper. Sift the flour with the salt. Beat the eggs with the sugar and instant coffee until very thick. Carefully fold in the flour and ground almonds. Do not overmix. Place the batter in the prepared cake pan and bake in a 375° oven 20 to 25 minutes or until a cake tester comes out clean. Cool the cake in the pan for 5 minutes and then turn out on a wire rack. Heat the preserves in a small saucepan and force through a sieve. Beat the cream until slightly thickened. Add the sugar and instant coffee and continue beating until thick. Split the cake in half. Spread one cut side with whipped cream. Top with the other half, cut side down. Brush the top and sides of the cake with strained apricot glaze. Arrange the drained apricots on top and brush them with the glaze. Press the ground nuts around the sides of the cake and sprinkle some on top.

Gateau Saint-Honoré

Gâteau Saint-Honoré

8 servings

Cream puff base:
 1 cup water
 ¼ teaspoon salt
 3 tablespoons sugar
 4 tablespoons butter
 1 cup sifted all purpose flour
 4 eggs

Filling:
 1½ cups heavy cream
 2 tablespoons sugar
 1 teaspoon vanilla
 ½ cup apricot preserves,
   heated and strained
 ½ cup sliced almonds

Decoration:
 3 tablespoons confectioners'
   sugar

Prepare the cream puff base following the directions for **cheese puff (see page 27)**. Using two spoons, form the mixture into a 9 inch circle. Bake on a buttered and floured baking sheet in a 375° oven for 30 minutes. Remove from the oven. Cool and cut in half horizontally. Whip the cream until it is slightly thickened. Add the sugar and vanilla. Sandwich cream between the 2 layers of the gateau. Spread the almonds on a baking sheet. Toast almonds in a 350° oven for 8 minutes. Cool the almonds. Brush the top layer of the gateau with clear warm liquid from the strained apricot preserves. Sprinkle with toasted almonds. Dust with sifted confectioners sugar.

Cheese cake

Tourteau fromage

6 to 8 servings

 2 egg yolks
 1½ cups sugar
 1 package (8 ounce)
   Philadelphia cream cheese,
   softened
 ½ cup butter, softened
   Grated rind of one lemon
 1 teaspoon vanilla
 1 cup sifted self-rising flour
 3 egg whites, stiffly beaten
 1 pint strawberries
 1 tablespoon Grand Marnier or
   other orange liqueur

Beat the egg yolks until they thicken slightly. Add ½ cup of sugar and beat until thick and lemon colored. Add the cream cheese and butter alternately with the remaining sugar, beating constantly. Beat in the lemon rind and vanilla. Fold in the flour carefully until just combined. Stir in ⅓ of the egg whites and fold in the remainder. Place the batter in a well buttered and floured 8 inch spring form cake pan. Tap the pan on the counter a few times to settle the batter. Bake in a 350° oven for 1 hour or until the cake tests done. Let cool in the pan 15 minutes before removing to cool further on a wire rack. Slice the strawberries and sprinkle with Grand Marnier. When ready to serve, place the cake upside down on a serving platter and top with the strawberries.

Apple pudding

Goueron aux pommes

4 servings

 4 medium sized cooking apples,
   peeled, cored and sliced
 4 tablespoons sugar
 ½ teaspoon cinnamon
 2 tablespoons brandy (optional)
 6 tablespoons butter
 ½ cup sugar
 3 eggs, lightly beaten
 1 teaspoon vanilla
 1 cup flour
 ½ teaspoon baking powder
 2 tablespoons confectioners
   sugar

Place apples in a 9 inch deep pie dish or 1 quart bowl. Sprinkle with sugar, cinnamon and brandy. Let the apples stand for 1 hour. Beat together the butter and sugar. Add eggs and vanilla and beat for 2 minutes. Fold in the flour and baking powder. Spoon this mixture over the apples and bake in a 375° oven for 35 minutes. Dust with confectioners sugar. Serve hot with ice cream or sweetened whipped cream.

Raspberry cake

Biscuits aux framboises

8 servings

- 4 egg yolks
- 4 egg whites
- ¾ cup sugar
- ¾ cup sifted all purpose flour
- ¼ cup butter, melted
- 1 teaspoon vanilla extract

Filling:

- ½ cup sugar
- ⅓ cup water
- 3 egg yolks
- 8 tablespoons butter, softened
- 2 tablespoons seedless black raspberry preserves

Decoration:

- ½ cup black raspberry preserves
- 1 package (1 tablespoon) unflavored gelatin
- ¼ cup cold water
- ½ cup sliced almonds, chopped finely

Beat together the egg yolks and sugar until very thick. Fold in the flour and the melted butter, adding a little of each at a time and folding the mixture over and over. Beat the egg whites until they stand in soft peaks. Fold egg whites into the egg yolk mixture. Pour into a buttered and floured 8 inch cake pan.

Bake in a 300° oven for 25 minutes until golden brown and lightly puffed. Remove the cake from the oven and allow it to cool. Split the cake into three layers. In the meantime, prepare the filling. Dissolve the sugar in the water. Place over high heat and boil until syrupy. (238 degrees on a candy thermometer.) Beat the egg yolks until thick. Continue beating while adding the boiling syrup slowly, in a steady stream of droplets. Continue beating until the mixture is thick. Beat the butter until softened. Beat the butter into the egg yolk mixture. Stir in the raspberry preserves. For the decoration: Sprinkle gelatin on the water and allow to stand undisturbed for five minutes. Heat the preserves and add the gelatin. Simmer until gelatin has dissolved. Allow the preserves to cool. Spread the bottom layer of the cake with most of the butter cream. Stack on the second layer and spread with the cooled jelly. Top with the third layer and spread with the rest of the cream. Spread the sides with the remaining jelly. Press chopped nuts around the sides of the cake. Cut into thin slices for serving.

Strawberry crêpes

Crêpes aux fraises

6 servings

1¼ cups milk
  1 egg
  1 egg yolk
  1 tablespoon butter, melted
  1 cup flour
 ¼ teaspoon salt
  2 tablespoons sugar
  1 (1 pint) box strawberries
     sliced
  2 oranges
  2 tablespoons sugar
  1 tablespoon Grand Marnier
  1 tablespoon butter
  2 tablespoons confectioners
     sugar, sifted

Place milk, egg, egg yolk,
butter, flour, salt and sugar in
a blender. Blend one minute until
smooth. Oil a crêpe pan and
and prepare crêpes following
directions for crêpes with honey,
page 76. Slice strawberries and
combine with grated orange
rind. Cut oranges into segments,
cutting between membranes.
Add orange segments, sugar
and Grand Marnier to
strawberries. Fill fruit into
crêpes and roll into cigarette
shapes. Place in a buttered baking
dish. Dot surface of the crêpes
with butter and bake 15 minutes
in a 350° oven. Dust with sifted
confectioners sugar and serve
hot with whipped cream or
ice cream.

Cream puffs with strawberries

Cream puffs with strawberries

Choux aux fraises

8 servings

Pastry base:
- *1 cup water*
- *4 tablespoons butter, cut into small pieces*
- *¼ teaspoon salt*
- *1 tablespoon sugar*
- *1 cup sifted all purpose flour*
- *4 eggs*

Filling:
- *1 cup sugar*
- *5 egg yolks*
- *¾ cup flour*
- *1 cup milk, simmering*
- *1 cup heavy cream, simmering*
- *1 teaspoon vanilla extract*
- *1 quart strawberries*
- *½ cup red currant jelly, melted*

Place water, butter, salt and sugar in a heavy saucepan. Adjust the heat so that the butter has completely melted when the water boils. Remove pan from the heat as soon as the water boils. Add the flour all at once and stir vigorously.

Return the pan to a moderate heat for two minutes until the dough can be formed into a ball. Remove the pan from the heat and add the eggs one at a time. Beat each egg well into the mixture before adding the next egg. Butter and flour two cookie sheets. Using 2 spoons form balls of dough about the size of an egg and place 3 inches apart. Bake in a 375° oven for 25 minutes until puffed and golden. In the meantime prepare the filling. Beat the sugar and egg yolks until thick and lemon colored. Beat in the flour. Stir in simmering milk and cream. Place in a saucepan over moderate heat and stir continuously to form a medium thick custard. Cool the custard. It will become thicker as it cools. Slice the top from each cream puff. Fill with cooled custard and top with strawberries. Brush strawberries with melted red currant jelly to make them shine. Decorate plates with remaining strawberries glazed with jelly.

Chocolate cake

Gâteau au chocolat

8 servings

Cake:
- *4 eggs*
- *¾ cup sugar*
- *3 squares (3 ounces) baking chocolate*
- *¾ cup sifted all purpose flour*

Butter Cream:
- *½ cup sugar*
- *½ cup water*
- *8 tablespoons unsalted butter*
- *3 egg yolks*

Decoration:
- *½ cup apricot preserves, melted and strained*
- *6 ounces dark sweet chocolate*

Butter and flour a 9 inch cake tin. Beat together the eggs and sugar until they are very thick. Break chocolate into pieces and put on a plate. Put plate on top of a saucepan of simmering water. Cover with another plate and allow the chocolate to melt. Fold ⅓ of the flour and ⅓ of the chocolate into the eggs and sugar. Continue alternating the flour and chocolate until well combined. Place in the prepared cake tin. Bake in a 350° oven for 45 minutes. Unmold and allow the cake to cool. Split the cake (horizontally) into 2 layers. Place sugar and water in a small saucepan. Boil 3 minutes until a thick syrup is formed (238° on a candy thermometer). Beat the egg yolks until thick. Continue beating the eggs while adding hot syrup in a slow steady stream. Beat 5 more minutes until very thick and doubled in bulk. Beat the butter until softened and lightened in color. Add butter to the egg yolks and syrup, a little at a time. Sandwich butter cream between 2 cake layers. Melt sweet chocolate between two plates set over a saucepan of simmering water. Line a cookie sheet with wax paper. Spread melted chocolate in a very thin layer on the wax paper. Chill chocolate 30 minutes. Brush the top and sides of the cake with the warm, clear liquid from the strained apricot preserves. Crumple the wax paper to break the chocolate into small thin wafers. Scatter chocolate wafers over the top and sides of the cake.

Raisin cake

Kougelhopf

10 to 12 servings

 1 cup butter
 5 eggs
2⅓ cups all purpose flour, sifted
 ½ teaspoon salt
 2 tablespoons sugar
 2 tablespoons lukewarm water
 1 package dry yeast
 1 teaspoon vanilla
 1 teaspoon lemon extract
 1 cup raisins
 ½ cup slivered almonds
 2 tablespoons powdered sugar

Beat the butter in a bowl until light and fluffy. Add the eggs one at a time and beat well. Add the flour, salt and sugar beating constantly. Dissolve the yeast in the water and beat into the dough along with the vanilla and lemon extract. Stir in the raisins. Butter a 10″ tube pan and sprinkle the bottom with the almonds. Turn the dough into the pan, distributing it evenly. Cover and let rise until the dough almost reaches the top of the pan. Bake in a 350° oven for 45 minutes. Let the kougelhopf cool in the pan for 20 minutes. Turn it out and sprinkle the top with powdered sugar. Cool thoroughly before slicing.

Aspic
A stiff gelatine obtained by combining fish or meat bouillon with gelatine powder.

Au gratin
Obtained by covering a dish with a white sauce (usually prepared with grated cheese) and then heating the dish in the oven so that a golden crust forms.

Baste
To moisten meat or other foods while cooking to add flavor and to prevent drying of the surface. The liquid is usually melted fat, meat drippings, fruit juice or sauce.

Blanch (precook)
To preheat in boiling water or steam. (1) Used to inactivate enzymes and shrink food for canning, freezing, and drying. Vegetables are blanched in boiling water or steam, and fruits in boiling fruit juice, sirup, water, or steam. (2) Used to aid in removal of skins from nuts, fruits, and some vegetables.

Blend
To mix thoroughly two or more ingredients.

Bouillon
Brown stock, conveniently made by dissolving a bouillon cube in water.

Broth
Water in which meat, fish or vegetables have been boiled or cooked.

'En papillote'
Meat, fish or vegetables wrapped in grease-proof paper or aluminum foil (usually first sprinkled with oil or butter, herbs and seasonings) and then baked in the oven or grilled over charcoal. Most of the taste and aroma are preserved in this way.

Fold
To combine by using two motions, cutting vertically through the mixture and turning over and over by sliding the implement across the bottom of the mixing bowl with each turn.

Fry
To cook in fat; applied especially (1) to cooking in a small amount of fat, also called sauté or pan-fry; (2) to cooking in a deep layer of fat, also called deep-fat frying.

Marinate
To let food stand in a marinade usually an oil–acid mixture like French dressing.

Parboil
To boil until partially cooked. The cooking is usually completed by another method.

Poach
To cook in a hot liquid using precautions to retain shape. The temperature used varies with the food.

Reduce
To concentrate the taste and aroma of a particular liquid or food e.g. wine, bouillon, soup, sauce etc. by boiling in a pan with the lid off so that the excess water can evaporate.

Roast
To cook, uncovered, by dry heat. Usually done in an oven, but occasionally in ashes, under coals or on heated stones or metals. The term is usually applied to meats but may refer to other food as potatoes, corn, chestnuts.

Sauté
To brown or cook in a small amount of fat. See Fry.

Simmer
To cook in a liquid just below the boiling point, at temperatures of 185°–210° Bubbles form slowly and collapse below the surface.

Skim
To take away a layer of fat from soup, sauces, etc.

Stock
The liquid in which meat or fish has been boiled together with herbs and vegetables.

Whip
To beat rapidly to produce expansion, due to incorporation of air as applied to cream, eggs, and gelatin dishes.

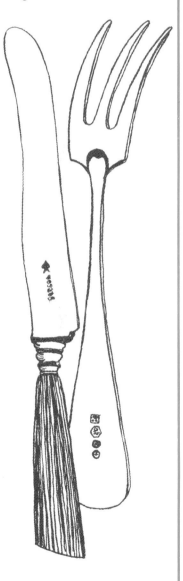

Conversion tables

Liquid measures

American standard cup

metric equivalent (approximately)

1 cup = $\frac{1}{2}$ pint	= 8 fl. oz. (fluid ounce)	= 2,37 dl (deciliter)
1 tbs. (tablespoon)	= $\frac{1}{2}$ fl. oz.	= 1,5 cl (centiliter)
1 tsp. (teaspoon)	= $\frac{1}{6}$ fl. oz.	= 0,5 cl
1 pint	= 16 fl. oz.	= 4,73 dl
1 quart = 2 pints	= 32 fl. oz.	= 9,46 dl

British standard cup

metric equivalent (approximately)

1 cup = $\frac{1}{2}$ pint	= 10 fl. oz.	= 2,84 dl
1 tbs.	= 0.55 fl. oz.	= 1,7 cl
1 tsp.	= $\frac{1}{5}$ fl. oz.	= 0,6 cl
1 pint	= 20 fl. oz.	= 5,7 dl
1 quart = 2 pints	= 40 fl. oz.	= 1,1 l (liter)

1 cup = 16 tablespoons
1 tablespoon = 3 teaspoons

1 liter = 10 deciliter = 100 centiliter

Solid measures

American/British

metric equivalent (approximately)

1 lb. (pound)	= 16 oz. (ounces)	= 453 g (gram)
	1 oz.	= 28 g
2.2 lbs.		= 1000 g = 1 kg (kilogram)
	$3\frac{1}{2}$ oz.	= 100 g

Oven temperatures

Centigrade	Fahrenheit	
up to 105° C	up to 225° F	cool
105–135° C	225–275° F	very slow
135–160° C	275–325° F	slow
175–190° C	350–375° F	moderate
215–230° C	400–450° F	hot
230–260° C	450–500° F	very hot
260° C	500° F	extremely hot

Index by type of dish

67 Duck with cherries
66 Duck with orange in aspic
65 Duck with prunes
63 Provençal chicken
64 Stuffed chicken or goose
   with apples
65 Stuffed guinea hen
67 Turkey from Poitou
66 Turkey in red wine sauce

Vegetable dishes

71 Asparagus with ham
70 Braised cabbage with
   chestnuts
70 Endives au gratin
69 Fried potatoes with
   cheese
69 Glazed carrots
69 Glazed onions
69 Green beans
68 Potatoes with cream and
   cheese
71 Pumpkin au gratin
72 Sautéed mushrooms
   country style
71 Stuffed mushrooms
71 Stuffed tomatoes Riviera
   style
70 Vegetable stew

Deserts

79 Apple omelette
86 Apple pudding
77 Baked cherries
73 Bavarian coffee-cream
79 Caramel custard
86 Cheese cake
78 Cherries in brandy
82 Chestnut block
89 Chocolate cake
73 Chocolate mousse
85 Christmas log
79 Cold lemon soufflé
81 Corn cake
89 Cream puffs with
   strawberries
76 Crêpes suzettes
76 Crêpes with apples
76 Crêpes with honey
80 Empress rice
81 Flambéed cherries
86 Gateau Saint-Honoré
75 Grand Marnier soufflé
83 Grape cake
86 Mocha cake
83 Normandy style apple pie
78 Peaches in white wine
79 Peach Melba
75 Pear sundaes
78 Pineapple flambéed in
   Kirsch

80 Plum compôte
90 Raisin cake
87 Raspberry cake
78 Strawberries Romanoff
88 Strawberry crêpes
85 Strawberry meringue
81 Sweet bread

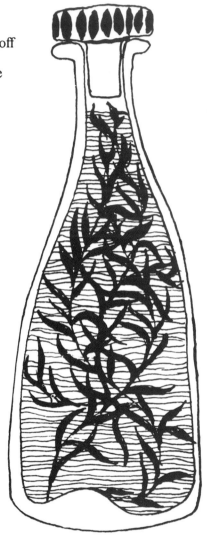